Homes on Wheels

Homes on Wheels

by Michael Aaron Rockland

photographs by Amy Stromsten

Rutgers University Press, New Brunswick, New Jersey

Library of Congress Cataloging in Publication Data

Rockland, Michael Aaron.
    Homes on wheels.

    Bibliography: p.
    Includes index.
    1. Van life—United States. I. Title.
GV1021.R54   796.7′9   80-20892
ISBN 0-8135-0892-4

cop. 1

For My Wife, Patricia Ard,
And For My Parents, Milton Rockland
And Bessie Sherry Rockland

Contents

Prologue

In the summer of 1977 I left New Jersey and drove West by myself. I had wanted to get away from it all, but most of the time I was miserably lonely. For comfort I kept a page torn out of a paperback copy of Robert Penn Warren's *All the King's Men* on the dash. It's the part where Jack Burden, finding his life falling apart all around him, heads West just like I was doing:

> I . . . went down to the bank and drew out some money and got my car out of the garage and packed a bag and was headed out. I was headed out down a long bone-white road, straight as a string and smooth as glass and glittering and wavering in the heat and humming under the tires like a plucked nerve. I was doing seventy-five but I never seemed to catch up with the pool which seemed to be over the road just this side of the horizon. Then, after a while, the sun was in my eyes, for I was driving West. So I pulled the sunscreen down and squinted and put the throttle to the floor. And kept on moving West. For West is where we all plan to go some day. It is where you go when the land gives out and the oldfield pines encroach. It is where you go when you get the letter saying: *Flee, all is discovered.* It is where you go when you look down at the blade in your hand and see the blood on it. It is where you go when you are told that you are a bubble on the tide of empire. It is where you go when you hear that thar's gold in them-thar hills. It is where you go to grow up with the country. It is where you go to spend your old age. Or it is just where you go.

It was just where I went. "Me and Burden," I kept saying to myself. "Me and Burden." Cowboys out on the range, moving to stay sane. Moving West where, as a professor of mine once said, "There are no problems. If you have a problem you take it out and shoot it."

Just after crossing the border into South Dakota, I spotted a caravan of strange-looking vehicles a couple of miles ahead. I couldn't tell if they were buses or trucks or what. No one was on the road but this caravan climbing slowly up into the Great Plains. For something to do, I put the pedal on the floor and went after them.

As I entered one of the few curves in that part of the country, the caravan, which was coming out the other end, was perpendicular to me. I could see large W's on the sides of the cratelike vehicles. What were they?

Then I remembered: Winnebagos! These were Winnebagos. I'd heard of Winnebagos and maybe I'd seen one before without it registering. But here was a whole wagon train of them—twenty, maybe twenty-five—lumbering along through the grasslands, heading West just like me.

Only the West seemed to mean something different to them than it did to me. I'd come out to lose myself in its vastness, but these folks were traveling to be together. As I approached the tail vehicle, a sign made up of tiny bulbs lit up in the back window saying "Howdy"; as I pulled alongside, kids waved to me through the curtained windows and the driver toasted me with a can of Coke; when I pulled in front the driver raised a microphone from the dash and spoke into it, sending word ahead about me on the CB.

I spent a full hour passing that caravan. I was in no hurry; I enjoyed the company. And company, hospitality, was what these folks were offering. These weren't mere travelers but an extended family, constantly jabbering to each other on the CB. They were on the road, but they were a community on wheels. As I passed each Winnebago, they greeted me like a stranger passing through their town.

Reluctantly, I approached the lead vehicle. As I passed and pulled in front, another sign of tiny bulbs flashed on and off. "COME AGAIN," it said.

I turned around and waved. "I will," I yelled out the window. "I will."

Homes on Wheels

Chapter I
Wheel Estate

These urges towards transience and mobility receive their ideal embodiment in that superlatively American invention, the house trailer, which is virtually nonexistent outside North America. Nomadism as a way of life, though not yet well documented by the social scientist, may have made marked progress during the 1960's.

Wilbur Zelinsky, *The Cultural Geography of the United States*

"Americans can't sit still. They're the movingest cusses I ever saw." Vernis Meyer was talking. He's an engineer at John Deere Tractors in Des Moines, Iowa. We met at an impromptu campsite in the hills outside Steamboat Springs, Colorado, later on in my western trip. I'd gone up there to look at a waterfall and decided to camp for the night. I was kind of nervous because no one else was around. There were no signs saying you couldn't camp, but there were none saying you could.

Pretty soon this big vehicle the size of a school bus came up the dirt road toward the falls, leaning first to one side and then to the other in the ruts. It pulled in next to me and out came Vernis, his wife Thelma, and four of their nine kids. Vernis questioned me about camping by the falls, as if I were an authority on the subject—though I had scarcely been there fifteen minutes. I was relieved when the Meyers decided to stay. Camping alone in an unauthorized spot, you're afraid someone will run you off; with two of you, there's already a tradition for them to contend with.

Vernis's rig was homemade. It was twenty-three feet long bumper to bumper, built up mostly of aluminum and fiberglass on a 1964 one-ton heavy-duty Chevrolet truck chassis that had been cut and stretched three feet. He had put in electrical and plumbing systems, a kitchen, bathroom with a shower, double bed in the back for him and Thelma, three-tiered bunk beds along the sides for the kids, closets, and a stereo sound system.

Building it was the culmination of a dream. "When I was a kid in the late 1930s," Vernis said, "I saw this converted bus at a truckstop in Great Bend, Kansas. It had everything in there—beds, a kitchen, a john. I said to myself, 'If ever I have a good job and some money I'm going to make me something like that.'" Vernis built his in his garage. When it was done it was one inch too high to get out of the garage, so he let the air out of the tires and his kids pushed it outside.

"In the beginning," Vernis said, "there hardly were any rigs like mine. Folks would see me coming and practically drive off the road."

When I met Vernis I thought his rig was pretty unique, too. Since then I've learned there are close to ten million American families, a full-blown subculture, cruising around in some kind of recreation vehicle—motor homes, vans, trailers, fifth wheels, pickup campers, converted buses, tent trailers, or homemades like Vernis's. Snowmobiles and motorcycles aren't considered recreation vehicles; nor are houseboats. Neither are mobile homes, though they were, years ago, before they became large and immobile. For something to be a recreation vehicle it's got to be part house, part motor vehicle, a traveling home on wheels.

Five hundred eighty-two thousand nine hundred of them, worth $4 billion, were manufactured in 1972, peak year for the industry (just before the Arab oil crunch). There are eight hundred or so RV manufacturers, the majority small outfits operating on the outskirts of towns in the Midwest, especially around Elkhart, Indiana. Some are so small they're in backyards and garages. Manufacturing RVs doesn't require a big investment and a lot of heavy machinery. Once you have the chassis, which are shipped from nearby Detroit, you build houses on them—carpentry mainly, some electrical work, some plumbing. The industry is a bastion of the cockeyed inventor-entrepreneur; it is the least unionized in America.

RV manufacturers have a national association called the Recreation Vehicle Industry Association, with headquarters in Chantilly, Virginia, just outside of Washington, a good spot for lobbying—essential in these days of fuel shortages. An RV industry Hall of Fame and museum will soon be set up at the University of Notre Dame in South Bend, Indiana, just down the road from Elkhart. RV owners also have their associations, with clubs for every kind of RV owner, thousands of local chapter publications, and a dozen national RV magazines. With the common problems of the road to unite them, RV people look after one another.

Usually, when someone has purchased an RV, he's hooked for life. He may trade up to something bigger or more elaborate—or, when the kids have grown, get a smaller, empty-nest RV. But once an RVer always an RVer. It's as if, by purchasing an RV, you've experienced some kind of conversion.

There are a million Americans living full time in RVs with no other home, gypsies by choice. They would have to be to afford homes that can cost as much as $100,000 and in some cases $200,000—even if they're on wheels. Probably it's because these homes *are* on wheels that most Americans, from the security of their foundation-anchored homes, tend to look down on them. If Americans look down on minorities who put their money into Cadillacs instead of "respectable homes," they're going to look down on RVers too. And now there's the moral justification of the energy crisis: "Not only are these people lowlifes; they're guzzling our gas." And for what? "To move their homes around the landscape instead of keeping them in place like normal people."

But there couldn't be a more normal guy than Vernis Meyer. Midwesterner, good husband and father, easygoing and kindly— an all-American. "Maybe," I found myself thinking, "it's the RV people who are the 'normal' Americans and the rest of us who aren't." Or, at least, maybe they represent something more typically American, more in touch with native American traditions. They're the ones who, like the immigrants and pioneers, have the courage to move; who discard outworn traditions without a backward glance; who, upon jumping into their RVs, escape the stagnant European past. It isn't accidental that the farther west you go the more RVs you see.

Vernis and I built a fire and stayed up talking half the night. The moon had come up. Below us you could see the lights of Steamboat Springs and to the east the dark forms of the front range of the Rockies. Mostly what we talked about was recreation vehicles. About how Americans are the most mobile people on the face of the earth but like to carry along hearth and home with them when they're on the road. "I'm no different than the pioneers pulling their covered wagons or the Indians

dragging their travois," Vernis said. "I like being on the move, but I like sleeping in my own bed every night, too. There isn't anything more American than a recreation vehicle."

John Steinbeck would have agreed. When Steinbeck traveled about the country in the early 1960s "to get in touch with America," and wrote the book about his experiences called *Travels with Charlie,* he lived in a pickup camper.

Steinbeck found Americans to be "a restless people, a mobile people, never satisfied with where they are as a matter of selection." After all, he argued, "the pioneers, the immigrants who peopled the continent, were the restless ones of Europe. The steady, rooted ones stayed home and are still there." Everywhere Steinbeck went he found people wishing they could be roaming around the country like him. They all had "a burning desire to go, to move, to get underway . . . to move about, free and unanchored."

No wonder so many Americans buy homes on wheels, the logical extension of these cravings. Not that the rest of us are far behind when you consider how we regard our automobiles. For most Americans, the automobile is not merely a vehicle; it is a second home. Or if not a home, a room. They eat and drink in it, listen to music, go to the movies, conduct their sex lives, sleep.

America's innovations in architecture have come in response to the automobile: suburbia, strip development, and drive-ins of all kinds—the drive-in movie, the drive-in bank, shopping malls, drive-in day care centers, motels, drive-in fast-food emporiums, and now even drive-in churches, where services are piped into every car and the collection plate is passed by attendants who walk between the rows of parked cars. The latest is drive-in funeral parlors, where you can view the deceased, propped up in a window, without getting out of your car. Only in America.

Because so much of our architecture derives from an automotive perspective, as opposed to the European's pedestrian perspective, our newer cities, like Las Vegas, resemble dragstrips. Although many Americans think Las Vegas represents all that is worst in our culture, it also can be thought of as representing what is most original. Tom Wolfe thinks Las Vegas is the only truly American city, "the Versailles of the United States." Buckminster Fuller would go even farther. He thinks architecture should be only temporarily placed on the land. Just as our planet travels through the heavens, so architecture should have the potential for movement from place to place, even on its own site—as is the case with Fuller's geodesic domes, Dymaxion House, and a quasi-recreation vehicle he designed, the Mechanical Wing.

In America there is a less distinct line between what is home and what is motor vehicle than in older, more traditional societies where homes are rooted in the soil. The typical American home features, if it does not enshrine, the garage, which takes up a great hunk of its floorspace. The mobile home, an assembly-line house on wheels that is towed to its site, could only have been the product of the American mind and of a homebuilding tradition that from its beginnings on the frontier necessarily accentuated the temporariness of wood over the permanence of brick and stone.

With such an overlapping of motor vehicle and home in the American imagination, small wonder America has spawned the giant recreation vehicle industry, for what home could be more temporary, more automobile-oriented—the ultimate "suburb"— than the recreation vehicle? Recreation vehicles are peculiarly American. If I could put only one American artifact into a time capsule, and had no restrictions as to size, it would be an RV.

The RV is a natural in a country that has always felt a conflict between its desire for stability, permanence, and roots, and its desire for mobility, change, and freedom. Homes with foundations might be a worthwhile goal but they also have connections to the feudal past. Clifford Holgrave, in Nathaniel Hawthorne's *House of the Seven Gables,* expresses it well: "But we shall live to see the day, I trust, when no man shall build his house for posterity. . . . It were better that they should crumble to ruin, once in every twenty years, or thereabouts, as a hint to the people to examine into and reform the institutions which they symbolize." Too bad Holgrave didn't build himself a recreation vehicle.

Sam Dodsworth did. The central character in Sinclair Lewis's *Dodsworth,* Sam is an early motor car manufacturer who quits the business and goes to Europe to please his wife, who has European pretensions. He tries to make a life for himself there, but it is no good; in Europe he discovers how much he is an American. He returns to America with plans to combine a new interest in architecture with a longstanding interest in automobiles—by manufacturing trailers. There seems no better way to reaffirm his Americanness than by building homes on wheels.

Recently I reread *Dodsworth* and realized that on my first reading I had overlooked the part recreation vehicles play in the story. I thought of how often I have seen recreation vehicles but blocked them out: the myriad roadside trailer salesyards; the campers detached from their pickups and standing in suburban driveways on their stilt-like jacks; the giant motor homes I have passed on the highway, wondering if they were some kind of bus; the multicolored vans chugging aggressively around the beach. Not to mention the political candidates I have seen operating from motor homes as mobile command headquarters; the rock groups and itinerant evangelists moving from one gig or camp meeting to the next in their bus-homes; Amy Carter repairing to the trailer set up as a comfort station behind the presidential stand where her father was reviewing the inaugural parade. I began to focus on the television shows to which recreation vehicles have been integral—Alan Funt's "Candid Camera," Charles Kuralt's presentations on CBS News, "Jean Shepherd's America," "Captain Marvel." And then there were the movies: The Desi Arnaz–Lucille Ball comedy, *The Long Long Trailer;* the Steve McQueen film *Junior Bonner;* the movie *Slither,* in which the bad guys, in black motor homes, chase the good guys in a silver Airstream; the Henry Fonda movie, *The Great Smokey Roadblock,* which features a band of prostitutes who,

furniture and all, move into and operate out of an eighteen-wheel truck headed cross country—thereby creating a peculiar kind of recreation vehicle and prompting an astonished sheriff to exclaim, "I thought I'd seen everything, but this beats all: a mobile cathouse!" All of these disparate experiences began to merge and take on importance for me.

My previous ignorance of recreation vehicles is understandable. They aren't part of the world of an eastern intellectual who lives in an ivy-covered house in an urban environment. They are almost *too* American.

I made an informal survey of friends and neighbors to test their familiarity with recreation vehicles. Of the twenty I questioned, only one truly knew what a recreation vehicle is. Two said "mobile homes," which, I suppose, was close. Four said "motorcycles" or "snowmobiles." Four said "dune buggies" or "four-wheel-drive vehicles." The others did not hazard a guess. RVs were as foreign to their world as camels, something to read about in *National Geographic.* In a way, this book is written for my interviewees. Next time they see these weird-looking vehicles moving down the highway, they'll know what they are.

They'll also understand their appeal: to carry around your home with you, like a turtle or a snail, self-contained, independent, a kind of backpacking writ large, wheeled, and luxurious. With an RV you can go anywhere and be fully equipped for whatever you find when you get there. And you can take along anyone you choose in your own Yellow Submarine.

RVs also appeal to the child in us. They have some of the same attraction as dollhouses and toy trains—the charm of the miniature world—except here the world is big enough to function in, big enough to *really* play house. RV people are fond of saying, "The bigger the boy, the bigger the toy." Maybe the difference between them and the rest of us is that they are unashamedly acting out these words.

In addition to being "toys," RVs are full of "toys"—that is, the same gadgetry found in luxury homes, usually scaled down: ice makers, microwave ovens, color TV sets, sophisticated stereo equipment, electric can openers, wet bars, built-in vacuum systems, air conditioners—you name it! The RVer's console of buttons rivals the cockpit of an airplane. As one manufacturer of recreation vehicles admits, "We built in so many gadgets, you'd have thought we were in the business of creating mobile display wagons for the appliance industry." Had the recreation vehicle industry gotten into high gear before energy became an issue, the space age gadgetry in RVs would by now be limitless.

Many Americans, observing luxury RVs, ask, "If that's 'roughing it,' how come it's fancier than my house?" To put their question another way, are RVs representative of a rugged frontier past or of a soft contemporary America? It may depend on the kind of RV and how it is used. Honest owners of luxury RVs make no pretense of being campers; they admit they are hedonists on wheels who enjoy the luxury of RVs in the same way others enjoy the luxury of yachts. RVs give them the ability to be footloose and fancy free while having a comfortable home along for the ride.

One of the pioneers of the industry, Wally Byam, who founded the Airstream Company, described RV life as "perfect . . . for spirited adventurers who want to roam—and take their armchairs with them." RVs, he writes in his book *Trailer Travel Here and Abroad,* are "compact apartments" on wheels. "Stepping into one is like stepping into your own home if it were shrunk to, say, 8' x 26' dimensions." They are so well equipped, you could turn one over to "your lovely old grandmother to tow out to the middle of the Sahara desert, confident that she could live in gracious comfort for a week or more without unloading, refueling, recharging—or regretting." For Byam, the joy of RV life is being on the road in a vehicle that has all life support systems aboard, one designed as carefully as those in which astronauts rode to the moon.

But while Byam celebrates the sophistication and gadgetry of modern RVs, he also constantly compares RVers with "the

"A rally is really a town temporarily set up in the 'wilderness.'"

frontiersmen and rugged individualists of the past," without seeing the contradiction. RV people seek the wide open spaces, but they like their comforts as much as the next guy. They talk about being out there alone on the frontier, but they're also the most gregarious people you'll meet. This becomes obvious at RV rallies and caravans, where individualistic values fade in the face of communal ones. At a rally, RVs are so close to one another it's difficult to connect what is going on with camping. A rally is really a town temporarily set up in the "wilderness" (often a large parking lot). But while each family lives in its own wheeled dwelling, the volume of human interchange and community organizing going on dwarfs that in any comparable American town. As soon as everyone arrives at the rally site, street signs go up, committees are formed, elections are held, potluck suppers are planned, classes are organized, amateur theatricals are rehearsed.

Certainly there are vestiges of the frontier at a rally. At many rallies, for example, RVs are parked in imitation of pioneer wagon formations. Wally Byam describes a rally at which "I thought of the old covered wagon trains and how they parked in a circle . . . in defense against Indians."

If rallies resemble halted wagon trains, caravans resemble wagon trains underway. Even the terminology is suggestive. The leader of the caravan, usually in the first vehicle, is called the "Wagon Master." The tail vehicle is considered to be "riding shotgun." Western terminology—"chow," "buckboard," "lawman"—crackles over the CB. But connections with frontier life are more symbolic than real. Caravanners aren't traveling in uncomfortable Conestoga wagons; they're in luxurious land yachts. They aren't facing hardships and dangers; they're traveling through the most affluent society in the history of the world. And they aren't alone; they're completely surrounded by people with whom they are in constant communication. A caravan is an ambulatory community.

Still, that wouldn't eliminate its ties with the frontier. Wasn't a wagon train also a community on wheels, its success dependent as much on cooperation as on individualistic exploits? Isn't our image of the frontier blurred by examples of reckless bravery on the one hand and quilting bees and barn raisings on the other? To put it another way, is it possible that, paradoxically, wagon train members never again experienced as great a sense of solidarity and community as when they traveled together?

Americans can't make up their minds whether the national character is basically individualistic or communitarian. Scholars are forever telling us either that we're incapable of meaningful association with one another or that we're on the verge of becoming conformist blobs. I'm not sure Americans suffer from either defect. Or maybe we suffer from a third: an extraordinary need to be both loners *and* joiners simultaneously. This would explain the appeal of recreation vehicles. Better than any artifact of our civilization, these hybrids embody both our individualistic and our communitarian instincts, our solitary and our gregarious ways, our desire to be free and on the road yet take our homes along with us.

They further embody our contradictory attitudes toward nature, our uncertainty as to whether we wish to dominate it or be one with it. From one perspective, recreation vehicles are the ultimate machine in the garden. From another, they are a reassuring example of the coexistence of technology and the pastoral ideal.

Vernis Meyer said it all that night several years ago, as the fire burned low and the darkness of the Colorado Rockies closed in. "What I like about my RV," he said, "is that I can get away from it all but have my family with me; I can be out in nature but have this rolling home with me. Let's face it," he concluded, "RVing is having your cake and eating it too."

Chapter II

The Immobilized Mobile Home

God Bless Our Immobile Home
plaque hanging in a mobile home

Movement intrigues the RVer, but so does comfort. In fact, RVers like their comfort so much that one kind of RV eventually became immobilized. In its evolution, the trailer reached a fork in the road: some trailers became lighter, sleeker, and more easily towable; others became heavier, more ponderous, and, eventually immobile. In this chapter we will look at the latter, a form of American housing with roots as an RV but which, each year, is becoming more like conventional American housing.

Three American Scenes

1—Just outside Elkhart, Indiana, a blue and white aluminum building nestles in the hollow under the embankment of the interstate. Inside, a black, wheeled structure eighty feet in length has been rolled through the cavernous door and placed crosswise in the assembly line. After a short pause, two gloved men, one on each end, push it to station one.

Soon an army of men in hard hats and canvas aprons are crawling over the chassis with power staplers. Great sheets of plywood are bolted in place for a floor. Alongside the line at station two, 2 x 4 studding is arranged in jigs and then lifted into place for wall supports. Further on down the line, sections of ceiling come off the jigs and are mounted, bats of insulation are unrolled and stapled into place, electrical and plumbing connections are made, sheet rock is nailed onto the studding, aluminum siding is fitted, a multi-layered roof sandwich is built up, windows and doors are hung. Now the behemoth is wheeled into a rain chamber where a hurricane pelts it. Inspectors with clipboards check for leaks.

After it emerges from the chamber, still being pushed along by hand—though it now takes four men to move it—paneling is brought in, linoleum for the kitchen area, carpeting, cabinets, toilets and baths, sinks, a dishwasher, a refrigerator, a stove, a washer and drier. Beds are brought in and set up, drapes are hung, a sofa, chairs, tables are selected and brought in, ceiling fixtures are wired into place, lamps are secured, a portable fireplace is placed under its stack.

More inspectors now, clipboards at the ready. Check. Check. Check. OK. The monstrous door at the end of the line is powered open. A tractor pulls another American home out into the sunshine. Time lapsed: 250 man hours of work. Price: $18,500 complete.

2—You're heading west on I-80 in central Pennsylvania. The traffic has spread out because of the mountains. The afternoon sun slants low into your eyes, making you sleepy, so you don't at first register the tractor trailer barreling toward you around a wide curve pulling a peculiar and extraordinarily long load. On one side it's finished, with white aluminum siding, chimneys poking up through the asphalt shingle roof. But the side facing you is open, covered with plastic, a blur of white appliances peeking through. It looks like somebody chainsawed off half a house and made off with it.

A mile up the road is another truck pulling what looks like the other half of the house. It is closed on your side but you can see loose plastic flapping on the other side.

Two halves of a double wide mobile home. Bathrooms, kitchen, furnace, all plumbing fixtures and major electrical installations on one side to cut down on expense. Bedrooms on the other side. Two halves of a house seeking a place to park, get bolted together, settle down.

Somewhere in rural Maine an American family, living in a tarpaper shack but doing better since John got the job in the paper mill, waits for their new home to show up. Price: $29,000 complete.

3—About twenty miles north of Orlando, Florida, unbeknownst to the thousands streaming toward Disney World, a rural exit off I-4 leads a couple of miles down a sandy road to a place called The Forest.

It is one of those planned developments—all the houses in dark cedar shingle, tropical plantings, bridges over little streams. Paradise.

If there have to be developments, this must be the nicest one in the world. The homes are huge, each with two and some with three wings. Some have pools, others lush patios. They're all different, except for the dark shingling—though this gives the development a pleasing unity.

Most of The Forest is already finished, but there's a new section being developed where you can see how the homes are put together and the landscaping done. I drive over and park next to a concrete block foundation. But wait, what's this? They're bringing in a section of a new house; it isn't being built on the site. And just beyond, a second and third section are parked in the dusty road. Workmen steer the first section into place on its foundation and begin to remove . . . the tires!

Unbelievably, this too is a mobile home. Luxurious, but mobile. Once it's in place, no one could tell. But if the owner ever chose to, he could unbolt the sections, attach tires, and move to another town, another state, another country. It costs one-third of what an equivalent stick-built house would cost because it's built on an assembly line and the materials for it are purchased on a mass basis. In this case, the company that owns The Forest also owns the factory where the homes are manufactured, so they can control the quality and the character of the homes from conception to installation.

These homes look as though they'd cost $150,000 easy. But in the office they say that the price is in the neighborhood of $50,000 for the most elaborate of the homes, with all furniture and appliances included. Of course if you don't want it furnished, it's cheaper. But I take a look at three or four of the homes and they're so tastefully done that, despite my independent ways, I would be hard pressed to keep from buying one of them as is.

A revolution in American housing? Or in American vehicles? Or both? Whichever, more than ten million Americans now live in mobile homes. In a little over a decade, between 1959 and 1972, conventional new home starts decreased from a little over a million to a little under a million a year, while mobile homes soared from one hundred thousand to five hundred thousand a year with a retail value of $4½ billion. In addition, several thousand specially equipped mobile homes are manufactured each year for use as temporary banks, construction site offices, schoolrooms, libraries, medical centers, and chapels. Mobile homes are increasingly being shipped overseas, where they have provided instant housing for Americans in such places as the Sinai buffer zone between the Egyptian and Israeli armies and at Saudi Arabian oil drilling sites. Skyline, the largest manufacturer of mobile homes, builds fifty thousand a year, more homes than the five largest builders of conventional homes combined—making it the number one American homebuilder by far.

In the 1970s, with inflation eating into the real earnings of the average American family, prices of conventionally built homes went up astronomically. Yet the traditional desire of Americans to own their own homes, even with the progressively smaller size of the family unit, has not diminished. For many, who otherwise might have only a stack of rent receipts to show for their efforts, mobile homes have been the solution. The already low prices of mobile homes are rising more slowly than those of conventional homes, and while older, vehicle-like mobile units depreciated rapidly, the newer, larger ones are tending to hold their own or even appreciate in value—like conventional homes. Today, up to 76 percent of housing starts of homes costing under $30,000, and up to 40 percent of *all* single family housing starts, are mobile homes. The industry slogan, "Affordable Housing for America," is becoming a reality.

The trend is likely to continue. Some years ago *Fortune* magazine argued that "the one sector of modern society that has remained largely unaffected by the industrial revolution" is the homebuilding industry. With the advent of large scale manufacturing of mobile homes, this is no longer the case. For the mobile home industry did not learn its methods from the construction industry; it learned them from the automobile industry. Mobile homes cost as little as they do because they are built in factories, where building materials, appliances, and furniture are bought en masse, and work is never halted because of inclement weather; there is also no pilferage, since materials and components are computerized and kept inside the factory building.

With the assembly line method of construction, innovations can be institutionalized rapidly. When energy first began to be a major factor, the industry made insulation of all surfaces standard, so that the mobile home today is by far the most energy efficient American home, saving as much as 50 percent on fuel costs over conventional homes of similar size. In 1979, smoke detectors became standard equipment in all mobile homes. That same year the first solar powered mobile homes rolled off assembly lines. Given its construction methods, the mobile home industry is able to introduce innovations rapidly while keeping prices low and profits high.

And to think it all originated in someone's desire to carry more tenting equipment with him on his automobile in the 1910s! Soon a larger luggage rack gave way to a wagon towed behind the car. This gave way, in turn, to the setting up of the tent on the bed of the wagon instead of on the ground (the ancestor of the pop-up tent trailer, which was being manufactured commercially by 1921). Finally, the idea was taken one last step: instead of using a tent, why not build a roof and sides on the wagon out of wood and metal? It wouldn't be necessary to set it up or take it down. There would be this little house traveling with you, available for use at any time, so you wouldn't have to stop traveling by a certain hour in order to make camp. Primitive, a kind of Thoreau's cabin on wheels, but a home nevertheless. Pulled by an automobile instead of a horse, but not much different than the Conestoga wagon of the pioneers. In fact, the first manufactured trailer was built in 1929 by a Detroit outfit called the Covered Wagon Company. It was nine feet long, six wide, had folding bunks, a coal burning stove, and was the grandmother of today's mobile home.

Many people use the terms "trailer" and "mobile home" interchangeably, but they are not the same thing anymore. One has become ever more useful for travel while the other has become ever more useful for living. So John B. Rae is in error in his book *The Road and the Car in American Life* when he says, "In America the covered wagon of pioneer days was a mobile home." It was a trailer. In *Trailer Travel Here and Abroad,* Wally Byam describes the moment when trailers and mobile homes split off and became distinct from one another. "On the one hand was a . . . group of manufacturers who had, from the beginning, believed that the trailer was essentially a vehicle for travel, a convenient instrument for comfortable vacationing. Little by little others appeared on the scene who seemed anxious to convert this truly *mobile* 'home' into a 'mobile' *home.*"

Initially, trailers met both purposes. During the Depression, they served as inexpensive housing for those moving from place to place seeking jobs. The very flexibility of their vehicle-homes also gave Depression trailerists a bad name. "Okies," "tramps," "gypsies," "tin can tourists" are words not entirely disassociated from RVers and mobile home dwellers to this day. Nevertheless, by 1936, trailer manufacturing was cited as the fastest growing industry in America, and one pundit predicted that within twenty years one-half of the population would be living in "automobile trailers."

During World War II, the government gave impetus to the industry by ordering thirty-eight thousand trailers for worker accommodations at war industry sites. Trailers were moved from factory to factory as need required. *Fortune* magazine described trailers as "the most promising form of instant low-cost housing since tents and caves and hollow trees."

After the war, trailers returned to being largely a novelty for those who enjoyed vacationing on the road. But there were others who had become habituated to the advantages and inexpensiveness of trailer housing during the war. They fed a market that built bigger and bigger trailers until they weren't trailers any more and a new term had to be invented for them: "mobile homes."

Wally Byam, a trailer man, did not welcome the advent of
mobile homes:

> These ungainly mutations, born of the travel trailer and
> sired by the housing shortage, could no longer be towed even
> by powerful Detroit cars. They were deposited at the edge of
> cities by equally huge trucks, like gigantic fixed eggs, never to
> move again. Cinder blocks were forced under them, flower
> beds appeared in the front "yards." As vehicles they were
> outside the restrictions of local building codes, and inspectors
> were powerless to condemn their wiring, plumbing, or flimsy
> construction.

What particularly disturbed Byam was that "the travel trailer
was punished for the offenses of its uncouth, earthbound
cousin."

It isn't any longer. As early as the 1950s, the distinctions
between trailers and mobile homes were becoming obvious as
the "earthbound cousin" became ever larger, luxurious, and
immobilized. Soon the only mobility new mobile homes enjoyed
on a practical basis was the trip from factory to homesite and,
occasionally, to another homesite, usually nearby. Only 2
percent of today's huge mobile homes will ever be moved again
once they have traveled to a homesite. When mobile homes are
sold these days they usually stay right where they are.

In 1955, the ten-foot-wide mobile home became standard, and
mobile homes ceased being "vehicles," since anything over eight
feet wide is illegal on American highways. Permits had to be
obtained to move "tenwides" down the highway, pulled by a
truck and blazoned with "WIDE LOAD" signs. By the 1960s, there
were twelvewides and by the 1970s, fourteenwides. In Texas
there are even some sixteenwides being manufactured. Lengths
also continued to expand: forty feet, sixty feet, eighty feet.
Today, the standard mobile home is eighty by fourteen—as much
floor space as a medium-sized ranch house. But some are far
larger. Increasingly popular are multiple section mobile homes,
which are joined on the site—doublewides and triplewides, as

well as L shapes, C shapes, and even E shapes. One manufacturer has experimented with multi-story mobile homes. While conventionally built homes have been getting smaller in recent years because of rising costs and other factors, mobile homes have been getting larger.

As the mobile home grew in size, its quality improved, but not in relation to its mobility. To put it another way, the mobile home was becoming less mobile, more home. While early mobile homes looked like elongated trailers, more recent ones added architectural features such as foundations, shutters, coach lamps, shingles, mansard roofs, bay windows, and even fireplaces. Mobile homes began to appear with model names like The Classic, The Colonial, The Cape Cod, and began to stress tradition in design rather than streamlining. Recent mobile homes have provisions for retracting or removing hitches and for totally disguising wheels with skirting of sheet metal, wood, or even brick. Mobile homes have become so attractive that home magazines such as *House Beautiful* have devoted spreads to them. This is fortunate because, whatever one thinks of mobile homes, their sheer numbers demand serious discussion as architecture.

As the size and quality of the mobile home continued to evolve, so did its name, for what had once been indistinguishable from trailers now had more in common with modular and prefabricated houses. In 1970, the United States Government included mobile homes as housing in the census for the first time. Then, in 1976, the industry officially adopted the term "manufactured housing" and its national organization outside Washington changed its name from the Mobile Home Institute to the Manufactured Housing Institute.

Until that time, the Institute had shared a building with the Recreation Vehicle Industry Association. This made sense in the past because of the overlapping history of RVs and mobile homes and because many manufacturers of one are also manufacturers of the other. As a major manufacturer of both states, "We have perfected a building system that profitably assembles components on a factory production line to turn out large quantities of low cost housing units known as mobile homes. Miniaturize the system and the product is known as a recreational vehicle." When the two organizations moved into separate buildings, it was as if they were formally disassociating themselves from one another over the question of mobility.

Mobile homes may have done so at their peril. One reason mobile homes far outsell modular and prefabricated homes is precisely because of their *potential,* however little utilized these days, for being moved from place to place should their owners desire. "The wheels, the wheels," Joe McGillicuddy, a California mobile homeowner explains. "That's what's so great about these babies. Just knowing that underneath the floor is a set of wheels makes you feel free." His neighbor, Horace Munn, adds: "If you don't like the temperature—if you don't like your neighbors—if you have even the most trivial reasons to move . . . you move."

Some mobile home owners actually decry the architectural features of contemporary models, preferring the more vehicle-like aspects of the older ones. It is more important that their "coach sleeps six" than that their mobile home has a Mansard roof. They like the mobile home's easy maintenance—the fact that it can be hosed down and waxed just like an automobile. They also like not having to pay real estate taxes and have agitated to "Keep the license plate on" (the vehicle license mobile homes must display). They criticize the elegant new mobile home parks, where mobile homes look like conventional homes to all but the most practiced eye.

The majority of mobile home owners, however, would prefer their homes to be indistinguishable from conventional ones. "For too many years people have thought of mobile homeowners as gypsies, wanderers, with no roots in any place," says Bob Andrews, a New Jersey mobile homeowner. "They can stop thinking that now because these are our homes." It seems inevitable that mobile homes will continue their drift away from recreation vehicles toward other forms of real estate. On balance, it is in the interest of mobile home owners. They would not have to finance their homes at exorbitant rates (since mobile homes are "vehicles" that can be driven away, banks will not finance them with home mortgages), they would not have to pay sales tax on them, and they would have a better chance of combatting anti-mobile home zoning.

As real estate, mobile homes are bound to have greater acceptance by, and impact on, American society. Perhaps as evidence of this, mobile homes have begun showing up more often in the media: in the television show "The Rockford Files," in the Broadway musical *Mary,* and in movies like *The Deer Hunter, Thunderbolt and Lightfoot,* and *Stroszek,* where German filmmaker Werner Herzog focuses on a mobile home as emblematic of the differences between life in the United States and life in Europe. Mobile homes have already changed the American landscape, with the mobile home parks of the 1970s now vying for a place in suburbia with the tract houses of the 1950s. Just as the suburban tract house was the means by which the middle class got to live "in the country," the mobile home is becoming the means by which Blue Collar America, as well as young marrieds and senior citizens on fixed incomes (the major groups who buy mobile homes), are doing the same thing. There are now some thirty thousand mobile home parks nationwide, and they have given rise to a new word—"Moburbia."

Mobile homes are here to stay. As Arthur Decio, Chairman of the Board of Skyline Homes has said, "The American Dream of homeowning is fast becoming the impossible dream, and until someone presents a viable alternative [to mobile homes] they are our best bet." To dismiss mobile homes and mobile home parks out of hand is difficult to square with our democratic traditions. A New York State planning official wrote in 1967: "If these so-called 'mobile homeparks' are allowed at all, keep them in commercial or industrial districts along major highways or down by the railroad tracks—preferably in swamps or abandoned gravel pits or as buffers between junkyards and gas stations." These elitist remarks conceive of mobile home park residents as subhumans who should be segregated from the rest of us by any means possible.

Of course, these comments were made well over a decade ago, and while there are still slum mobile home parks today ("tin ghettos" as they are called), others look more like country clubs. They have clubhouses, pools, shuffleboard, and other athletic facilities. People live in them not because they have to; on the contrary, there are long waiting lists to get into them. One reason is that mobile home parks offer community life unparalleled in today's America. The mobile home park is the closest thing to what small town life was early in this century. As one mobile home park resident said to me, "Here if you get sick, people care." And as another said, "It's like being back on Main Street again. Everyone's friendly. You can leave your door unlocked. Who wants to live out there?" she asked, pointing beyond the gates of the park.

The gates (and fence) suggest another reason why, for many, mobile home parks are the residence of choice. In every survey of mobile home park residents, many of whom are elderly, the same refrain, *security,* is heard. Mrs. Charles Moore, an elderly woman who lives in Santa Rosa, California, writes me that "Our primary concern in coming to a mobile home park was protection of property and person." Mobile home parks are, in effect, private towns to which entry is restricted, keeping them apart from the general society while creating solidarity within.

Still, many mobile home owners prefer not to live in a park but on their own land. In some states, particularly in the populous Northeast, this is often impossible because of zoning, which keeps mobile homes restricted to parks. As one New Jersey mobile homer said to me, "Getting a permit to put a mobile home on your own land in New Jersey is more difficult than getting a liquor license."

But in less congested states, where zoning is not restrictive, many mobile home owners live on their own land. When John Steinbeck traveled about the country in his pickup camper in 1960, he found many mobile homes on farms. Said one farmer to Steinbeck, "I'm tired of living . . . with the wind whistling through, tired of the torment of little taxes and payments for this and that. It's warm and cozy [in his mobile home] and in the summer the air conditioner keeps us cool." While it used to be customary to build rooms onto a farmhouse when new babies arrived or children married, today a mobile home is often placed on the land at some distance from the main farmhouse—a way to preserve some of the advantageous vestiges of the extended family without the disadvantageous ones. "Each family has a privacy it never had before," Steinbeck writes.

> The old folks are not irritated by crying babies. The mother-in-law problem is abated because the new daughter-in-law has a privacy she never had and a place of her own in which to build the structure of a family. When they move away . . . they do not leave unused and therefore useless rooms. Relations between the generations are greatly improved. The son is a guest when he visits the parents' house and the parents are guests in the son's house.

Mrs. Alva Johnson, an elderly widow with sixteen grandchildren and three great grandchildren, lives by herself in a mobile home on a rural road near Bucksport, Maine. Several of her children live with their families in mobile homes ten and twenty miles away. Mrs. Johnson will have no part of mobile home parks. "I hate them," she says. "I've seen a lot of them in Florida and California. The houses are too close together. You can hear the toilet flushing in the next trailer. A man and his wife can't have a conversation without everyone hearing. I get a lot of snow and frozen pipes, but I'd still rather be on my own. It's lonely, but I've got to have my independence."

Mrs. Johnson's independence of spirit is reflected in the values and attitudes of the mobile home industry as a whole. It mistrusts government and, along with its sister, the recreation vehicle industry, is among the least unionized in America. This is partly due to its being headquartered in Elkhart County, Indiana, where the high concentration of enormously productive Amish and Mennonite farmer-workers is opposed to unions and governmental assistance of any kind on quasi-religious grounds. Workers in the industry are paid high wages but have few fringe benefits. If there is a layoff, they go back to farming for a while. They have no consciousness of being an industrial proletariat. Some are thinking, "Maybe I can have my own factory someday." Says Keith Meade, Executive Director of the Elkhart Chamber of Commerce, "The mobile home and RV industry is the epitome of the American free enterprise system. People go in and out of business overnight. Two guys get together—one with some manufacturing experience, the other with some marketing experience—and the next day there's a new mobile home or RV brand being manufactured in a third guy's backyard."

Like the recreation vehicle industry, the mobile home industry functions in a boom/bust cycle not unlike wildcat oil companies. According to Meade, "RV and mobile home people are grasshoppers, not ants. They feast in summer and lay nothing aside for winter—personally and corporately. They are Go-Go types." Elkhart is known as the town with the greatest percentage of self-made millionaires in America. Says Keith Snelson, who quit a vice presidency with a major corporation to manufacture a tent trailer small enough to be pulled by a motorcycle, "There are more entrepreneurs in this town per square foot than anywhere in the world. Everyone in Elkhart shoots from the hip."

Surprisingly, many Americans have never heard of Elkhart. A Fort Wayne, Indiana schoolteacher with whom I spoke obviously had heard of Elkhart but didn't know that it was the center of the RV-mobile home industry—which is the equivalent of someone living seventy-five miles from Detroit and not knowing that motorcars are manufactured there. Elkhart has an affinity for Detroit: not only do its chassis come from there but the bustle of its many young industries is often compared with the Detroit of the 1920s. Day and night, freight trains move in and out of Elkhart, feeding the town's 450 factories. One out of every three of Elkhart's fifty thousand men, women, and children are employed in manufacturing. Elkhart is a flourishing example of an America some commentators on the "post-industrial" era assert has disappeared.

Elkhart's story is the story of Arthur Decio, one of its native sons and Chairman of the Board of the Skyline Corporation, the nation's largest manufacturer of mobile homes and its third largest manufacturer of recreation vehicles. Skyline has come all this distance since 1952, when Decio returned from college to take over the tiny trailer factory his Italian immigrant father, who owned a bar in Elkhart, had established as a sideline in the garage behind the family home. From only one unit per week, Decio built Skyline into a $400,000 per year corporation, with mobile home and recreation vehicle factories all over the country. In 1965, when Decio was only thirty-four, he already had a personal fortune of $5,000,000 and had been featured on the cover of *Time* magazine. The United States is still "the best place for a man to make his million," said *Time.*

Decio is an extraordinarily dynamic person who works long hours and is known throughout the industry as "a one-armed paper hanger." "I try to pull Skyline instead of pushing it," he says. "Everyone works here." At corporate headquarters in Elkhart, one is surprised by the smallness of Skyline's central staff and by how little bureaucracy there is. The corporation doesn't even have a public relations department; one has to talk to Decio himself—which is easier said than done. Keith Meade, of the Elkhart Chamber of Commerce, told me it once took him two years to reach Arthur Decio by phone. I thought he must be exaggerating until I had a similar experience: I tried for a year and a half to speak with Decio and made two unsuccessful trips to Elkhart. Then, one day, the phone rang in my home in New Jersey. I was out in the driveway shoveling out from under a blizzard. Racing into the house, I picked up the phone and a voice said: "Hello, Mike? This is Art."

"Art who?" I snapped.

"Art Decio," he replied. "I hear you've been trying to reach me."

Art Decio is proof that the self-made captain of industry is still alive in America. There are overtones of a personality cult in the way Decio's name and face are plastered over everything Skyline does. He is famous in the industry both for his kindness and his rages, during which he purportedly overturns furniture and tears phones off the wall in his office. When a young Democratic politician he was supporting for office showed up late for a fundraising party Decio was throwing for him, Decio took him firmly by the arm and steered him into his study before introducing him to anyone. "Senator Bayh and Congressman Brademas never come late to my house," Decio informed the by then trembling young man.

Decio has a reputation in the industry for being tough but honest. He is also its key spokesman and moral philosopher. "Some years ago, builders just decided to forget about low-income groups," he says. "This was our opportunity. . . . Although there are a lot of steakeaters, the basic diet is still hamburger." Decio speaks with missionary zeal for what the mobile home industry is doing. "It is within our power," he says, "to resolve the paradox that has the richest nation in the world unable to provide . . . housing for its people." It was Decio who gave the industry its slogan, "Affordable Housing for America," which can be seen on bumper stickers around the nation.

Decio's ideas are spread through "The American Dream in Housing" show which is regularly performed at mobile home and recreation vehicle expositions. A cutaway Skyline mobile home is used as a stage set, with the action moving through the various rooms of the house. The show is a short musical comedy—with songs and choreography. The argument of the show is that "The story of America is really a chronicle of man's unending quest for home ownership," a quest that now "is in jeopardy." "What's happening in America?" one song asks. "What's happened to the American dream? The dream of Jefferson, that each American might have his own home?" What's happening, the show goes on to demonstrate, is that 85 percent of the American people can no longer afford conventional homes.

Mobile homes to the rescue! Mobile homes, that wedding of democracy and technology, the people's homes, "the red, white, and blue invention." No more renting—that feudal institution. No more trying to buy a home you can't afford. In a final song, "You American Dreamers," the singers tell the audience that "Skyline dreams the American dream."

Corny as it is, the show gives you goose bumps. It is also enormously effective at convincing an audience that a mobile home is solid and attractive on the one hand and inexpensive and nearly tax free on the other. And then there's one more thing: a mobile home can be moved. Beneath the attractive furnishings, the bright lights, the glamorous smiles of the young dancers and singers, there are still wheels.

Chapter III

Covered Wagons: Wally Byam and the Airstream Company

I was standin' dere, my thumb out, in Arizona I tink, mindin' my own business, when dis blindin' white stuff appeared way down the highway. I couldn't tell in da settin' sun whether it was a lightnin' storm or a band of angels. "Holy Jesus," I says to myself. Well it all starts coming towards me, so I backs away from the highway. Soon de're all going by: Phwap. Phwap. Phwap. Phwap. Maybe fifteen-sixteen of dem. Just like dat. An den I seen da names on dem: "Airstream."

Joe Morris, an old hitchhiker, as taped by the author

"Wally's act was such a tough one to follow, anyone in this job, no matter how creative, would tend to be more of a perpetuator than an innovator." Charles Manchester, president of the Airstream Company, was speaking. He was talking about Wally Byam, founder of Airstream and the inventor of the Airstream trailer, the silver bullet of the American highway. If ever a corporation could be called the lengthened shadow of one man, it is Airstream.

Wally Byam's Airstream is proof that while "trailers" were evolving into "mobile homes" which, in turn, were giving way to "manufactured housing," trailers themselves also continued to evolve. As mobile homes became less mobile, trailers became more so—increasingly lightweight, with space-age suspension and towing systems. Though new kinds of recreation vehicles— motor homes, pickup campers, vans—have come along, sales of trailers have continued to approximate those of all other recreation vehicles combined. In 1972, the industry's biggest year to date, 250,000 trailers were sold out of a total RV sale of 582,900—not including fold-down and tent trailer sales of 110,200 (though the figure does include fifth wheels, the largest and newest type of trailer, whose front fits into the bed of a pickup truck). For some Americans, recreation vehicles and trailers are synonymous.

One reason for the continued popularity of trailers is that the tow vehicle is separable from the trailer. Motor homes, vans, and pickup campers are integrated units—and there is certainly a convenience in that. But the instant detachability of the trailer means that the driver of the tow vehicle is free to go wherever he wishes, unencumbered by his home—an important advantage in these fuel scarce times. As one full-time trailerist put it to me, "Who wants to drive to the store for a loaf of bread in a huge motor home which only gets three miles to the gallon and with everything bouncing around inside? I leave my trailer where it is, and if we're camping, that reserves my spot." This trailer owner estimates he drives twenty thousand miles a year, only ten thousand of them with the trailer attached. "Can you imagine what I save on fuel on the other ten thousand?" Also, he points out, "If something goes wrong with the car, I have the trailer to live in while it's being fixed. If the trailer needs fixing, I've got the car. If I had a motor home, both my vehicle and my home would be out of commission if anything went wrong with either part."

The leader of the trailer industry for virtually as long as anyone can remember has been the Airstream company. Not that Airstream has led in sales. It is, rather, its engineering advances and, particularly, its recognizability, or generic quality, that cause many Americans to picture an Airstream when the word "trailer" is mentioned.

Like many pioneers in the recreation vehicle industry, Wally Byam built his first trailer in his California backyard just for fun. "In those days [the late 1920s] even amateurs could put together what we considered a very handsome vehicle with materials available in a junkyard and hardware store. The whole cost wouldn't run to more than a hundred dollars . . . an old Ford chassis, a few sheets of plywood, some masonite, nails and bolts, plus whatever accessories you could afford—a second hand sink, gasoline stove, an icebox, and the bed could very well be an old mattress stretched out on the floor."

Proud of his trailer, Wally wrote an article about it for *Popular Mechanics* magazine. So much mail came in response that he converted the article into a little booklet which sold well. Soon "several people wanted me to build trailers for them instead of merely telling them how to do it." Before long, Wally was "head over heels in orders," and, in 1930, he "closed out the publishing business and went into the trailer business."

The widespread use of aluminum in the aircraft industry had as a by-product the first all-aluminum Airstream built by Byam in 1937. It was immediately popular. The strength and durability of aluminum trailers is demonstrated by the fact that some of those first Airstreams are still on the road. World War II soon intervened, however, and aluminum was not available. "Always the purist," as Charles Manchester describes him, Wally suspended production for the duration of the war and put his engineering skills to work for Lockheed Aircraft. Then, with the war over, and aluminum available again, he started up Airstream production on a greatly expanded basis, first on the West Coast, then in Ohio, where two-thirds of Airstream's production now is.

Despite Airstream's success, Wally was no businessman. Twice he went broke, and had it not been for the talents of his principal officers in California and Ohio, Airstream might have folded. Charles Manchester tells the following story:

> Years ago I was at a rally with Wally. There was a doctor there who had had a lot of trouble with his trailer. He grabbed Wally and roasted him about the efficiency of Airstreams. Wally turned to me and said: "Give this man his money back. We don't want him in the organization." I didn't want to give him his money back; we weren't that financially solvent. But Wally thought this man didn't *deserve* an Airstream.

Where Wally's talents lay were in leadership. Frank Judy, manager of Airstream's plant in Jackson Center, Ohio, remembers Wally coming to Ohio from the California plant with a flatbed truck loaded with the makings of a sample trailer. That was all they had when they got started in Ohio. But, says Judy, "Wally made a lot of decisions and he made them fast. Not long after we got started, he was inspecting the assembly line and found a minor defect in a particular trailer. He tore the furniture out of the trailer, threw it on the ground, and stomped on it. We never made that mistake again."

Wally's quick temper was softened by his openness. "He was the kind of guy who talked with everyone," says Bob Ambrose, dispatcher at the Jackson Center plant. "He made everyone feel necessary and important—even the plant sweepers. Everyone called him 'Wally.' " This part of Wally's legacy has carried over to Charles Manchester. Throughout the company he is referred to simply as "Chuck." "Chuck says" and "Chuck thinks" is the way people throughout the company begin many of their sentences.

Wally's charisma as a leader was enhanced by his dress and life-style. Never without Wellington boots and the blue beret which is now worn by Airstreamers everywhere, Wally lived much of the year in his custom, gold-anodized Airstream—camping on the factory grounds when he visited the Ohio plant. He always insisted that his "enthusiasm for traveling by trailer took precedence over my commercial interest in them." Wally traveled thousands of miles every year in his trailer, sometimes alone, sometimes leading caravans, always evangelizing for Airstream.

I say "evangelizing" because Airstream seems as much faith as product. All company literature includes "The Wally Byam Creed," which Airstream owners joining the Wally Byam Club recite, right hand raised. Tom Haapala, new with the company as director of public relations, said to me, "I'm never sure when what I'm doing in this job is business or religion"; Tony Hilgefort, regional sales coordinator, refers to Wally as "The Force." Calvin Trillin, writing about an Airstream caravan in *The New Yorker,* found that "Some followers of the late Wally Byam . . . are almost as devoted as some followers of Karl Marx or Adele Davis or Baba Muktananda."

The quasi-religious aspects of Airstream contribute to its esprit. There isn't a company or product in America where manufacturer, dealers, and customers are so wedded to one another. "Here at the company you feel part of a family," Tom Haapala says. Dealers also have a special affection for the product they sell: many Airstream dealerships are "Mom and Pop" operations which began with the purchase of a personal trailer purely for vacation purposes. Airstream owners rave about the courtesy and care with which they are treated and the factory grounds at Jackson Center are covered with Airstreamers who have stopped for repairs or are just camping for a few days at "home base." During the energy crisis of 1973–1974, Airstream officials manned phones around the clock, delivering small quantities of gasoline to stranded Airstreamers anywhere in the United States.

Airstreamers consider their RVs "the Cadillac" or the "Rolls Royce" of the industry and take satisfaction in owning one, as well as enjoying a measure of social status. "I don't care if other RVers are jealous of me," one Airstreamer said to me. "I've got *quality* here." An index to the quality of Airstreams is the fact that, until prohibited recently by federal regulations, the company warranted them for life.

Airstream makes no bones about the fact that its trailer, with all its luxury, has more "travability" than "liveability." The standard, box-shaped trailer has more room and, without curving walls, may be more comfortable once parked. But it isn't built to last, its towing and mileage performance is inferior. Also, since it is much heavier than the aluminum Airstream, it requires a larger towing vehicle. Airstream is the only large trailer that can be pulled by any American six-cylinder car—which should help its chances of survival in the energy crunch.

Airstream has always calculated its appeal from an engineering standpoint. Company stationery sports a logo of a man on a bicycle towing an Airstream, while sales brochures show workmen picking up whole sections of the trailer with one hand to demonstrate its light weight and other workmen chinning themselves on sections of the trailer to demonstrate its strength. With the energy crunch, Airstream ads emphasize its aerodynamic shape even more than in the past. While most trailer manufacturers admit that towing a large trailer will halve gas mileage, Airstreamers insist there is only a 3 MPG difference between driving with the Airstream in tow and driving without it. The thirty-one foot Airstream weighs 4950 pounds, no more than some Oldsmobiles. Other trailers of the same length weigh as much as 7500 pounds. Airstream owners are fond of telling stories about driving off without remembering to hitch up their lightweight homes and being unaware they had left them behind until they were many miles down the road.

Airstream's engineering is demonstrated by the many special uses to which the trailer is put. The King of Morocco buys two or three Airstreams every year, as did the Shah of Iran. Many

Airstreams are bought in developing parts of the world, jungles and deserts, where immediate, self-contained housing is required and mobile homes are too large to be brought in or road conditions are so bad that a less well-engineered trailer would fall apart in transit. Airstream's water purification systems also make them useful in areas of the world with poor health conditions. There is actually an Airstream dealer in Kuwait, and while I was at company facilities in Ohio, an Arab businessman to whom Airstream expected to sell several trailers was visiting.

Because of the quality built into them, Airstreams have been used by universities as mobile laboratories and by governments for special projects. The Canadian Defense Department recently purchased two Airstreams for use in a laser gun project. The American Secret Service owns several and uses them as mobile command centers during political conventions. Those silver decontamination stations used by astronauts on their return from the moon were custom Airstream trailers which were installed aboard the recovery ships with wheels removed.

Airstream's quality and engineering make it one of the few recreation vehicles that depreciates slowly, if at all. Also, only slight changes are made in the external appearance of the trailer from year to year—guaranteeing, as a company brochure states, "no planned obsolescence." Indeed, some Airstream owners claim to have been able to sell their trailer for what they paid for it years later or for even more—which makes Airstreams function somewhat more like homes than vehicles in the economic market.

This is how many Airstreamers see their trailers: as homes. Dr. Kenneth A. Estabrook, a retired Airstreamer from California, writes me: "What a wonderful world we have to live in—to explore and . . . to enjoy, always with the comforts of our own home." When Estabrook and his wife travel, they tote along a spinet type Hammond organ in their trailer and give impromptu concerts wherever they stop for the night.

Because of its home quality, Airstream is the trailer of choice

"with the comforts of our own home."

for those people who are known in recreation vehicle circles as full-timers. Kay Peterson, author of *Home Is Where You Park It,* a recent book about living full-time on the road, owns an Airstream. In her book, Mrs. Peterson devotes several pages to why she and her husband chose an Airstream trailer to live in when they adopted a full-time RV life-style. "We decided on . . . [it] because we believed it would better endure the tests of time and constant use. Then, too, Joe is convinced it tows better because of its aerodynamic design." Gran Roe, a New York City high school teacher told me he and his wife Judy, also a teacher, plan when they retire to live full-time in their Airstream on the road. "I've owned three other kinds of trailers before this Airstream," Roe says, "and they fell apart before my eyes. This one just seems to get better as time moves along."

Among the hundreds of companies in the recreation vehicle business, only Airstream inspires such loyalty among its customers, most of whom will never buy another kind of RV. This is only in part because of the virtues of the product itself. Calvin Trillin writes: "Most of the people I met on [the] Caravan . . . said they chose an Airstream mainly for the programs that surround it." And an Airstreamer told me: "My husband and I bought an Airstream not because we think it's all that much better. In fact, given what it costs (about $19,000 for our 31 footer), dollar for dollar it *isn't* any better. We bought an Airstream because of the Club."

The club referred to is the local chapter of the Wally Byam Caravan Club International, the main activity of Airstream's Way of Life Department, which administers the "after purchase benefits program." An Airstream official sees the Way of Life program as "designed not only to encourage the purchaser to use the product, but also to have fun after he bought it." The statement probably differs little from that any corporation executive might make in reference to his product. The difference with Airstream is that the Way of Life Department is central to what the company does and integral to its success.

The Way of Life Department is the company's communications link to Airstream owners, who usually remain in contact with the company for as long as they own an Airstream—which, for many, is the rest of their lives. And Airstreamers are the best public relations people a company ever had. They are forever saying, "There are no strangers in Airstream: there are only friends who haven't met yet," and celebrating the fact that wherever they go they feel part of the Airstream fellowship. "It doesn't matter where you stop," an Airstreamer said to me; "sometime during the night another Airstream will pull in next to you." Airstreamers more closely resemble lodge brothers than explorers.

One thing that makes for conviviality among Airstreamers is the large red numerals on their trailers. When Airstreamers approach one another on the highway they immediately look up the other trailer's occupants by number in the club directory and salute them. The directory also indicates which members around the country offer free parking and even hookups in their driveways or backyards. As one Airstreamer put it to me, "It's really something to knock on someone's door in a strange town and, as soon as they know you're an Airstreamer, they greet you like a long lost friend."

One Airstreamer (#29581) was inspired to write a poem about the red numbers and about the Wally Byam Caravan Club International (abbreviated WBCCI) crest which decorates each Airstream:

"THOSE RED NUMBERS AND THAT CREST"

When I'm traveling down the highway,
And I'm far away from home,
Though I'm in a crowd of travelers,
Yet, somehow, I feel alone.
Then I drive down through a valley
And up around a bend;
I meet an Airstream with red numbers;
And I know I've met a friend.

. . . .

It is great, when you are traveling,
To know that you belong
To a club that's International,
Whose members all love fun and song,
Who will help you, when in trouble,
Will never leave you high and dry;
And those numbers and that Crest just say,
"We're W.B.C.C.I."

Airstreamers take their club numbers very seriously indeed, signing letters and otherwise identifying themselves with their WBCCI numerals in addition to their names. Great prestige in Airstream circles is associated with a low number—which signifies that the individual towing that trailer is one of the original Airstreamers, close to Wally himself who was, of course, #1. The company directs dealers to remove numbers from traded in Airstreams so that purchasers of used trailers do not accidentally get a low number. The company tells dealers, "It is very upsetting to our owners when 'their' number is seen on someone else's trailer."

Wally Byam organized the WBCCI in 1955 and it now has 160 local units, some twenty-seven thousand trailers registered, and over sixty thousand individual members. The club publishes *The Blue Beret,* a monthly magazine with information on legislation affecting RVs and lobbying efforts on their behalf—as well as news of upcoming national and regional caravans and rallies.

Wally Byam conceived and organized the overseas caravans for which Airstream is famous. Byam liked to think of himself as a world statesman, and company literature always pictures him with a globe beside him and never fails to mention his vision that Airstreamers traveling abroad carry with them "a cocoon of our civilization." The Wally Byam creed includes this oath: "To play some part in promoting international good will and understanding among the peoples of the world and through person-to-person contact." The company augmented its internationalist image in recent years by donating Airstreams to

the State Department to be used for re-Americanization trips of
American Foreign Service families and for taking foreign
journalists and diplomats around the country during the
Bicentennial celebration.

In 1955, Byam organized the 500 Caravan to Mexico, so-called
because over five hundred Airstreams made the trip. The
Mexican caravan trip has been repeated many times, and a
regular staple of it is the piggybacking of the entire caravan on
flatbed railroad cars for the trip over some of Mexico's highest
mountain ranges, everyone traveling in their own RV for days
without using gasoline. *Life* magazine thought the 500 Caravan so
unusual they flew down and shot it from the air. Since then, the
Way of Life Department has organized caravans throughout the
United States, Canada, Central America, and even overseas to
Europe (the trailers being loaded on ships like containerized
cargo). In 1960, shortly before his death, Byam led a caravan the
length of the African continent, from Capetown to Cairo.

The great majority of those participating in the caravans are
elderly and retired people who seem to get a new lease on life
through adventure. Tom Wolfe describes an Airstream caravan
in his essay "The Me Decade and the Third Great Awakening"
as a way to "cut through the whole dreary humiliation of old
age." Instead of vegetating and getting crotchety, elderly people
("the Gerontoid Cowboys," Wolfe calls them) join a convoy of
"thirty, forty, fifty Airstream trailers . . . hauling down the
highway in the late afternoon" while "various rheumatoid
symptoms disappear, as if by magic." Instead of feeling sorry for
themselves, they look at their workaday children "as sad
conventional sorts whom they had left behind, poor turkeys who
knew nothing of the initiations and rites of passage of
trailering."

Wolfe thinks a caravan may be more of a community than
those its members left behind. It is also a tonic for old age, an
active retirement rather than a cessation of activity. Chuck
Manchester says Airstream consciously appeals to "an older age
group—people who need challenges, friendships, adventure. Our

caravans give them a purpose." Concludes Calvin Trillin: "For a lot of the Airstreamers, traveling in a caravan is not principally a way to deal with the difficult business of traveling but a way to deal with the even more difficult business of being retired."

Rallies serve a similar function for Airstreamers. People find jobs for themselves reenacting their preretirement roles. Everyone has something to do—laying out streets, handling parking, organizing garbage and "honey bucket" (sewage) details, setting up a first aid station, arranging for grocery delivery, organizing entertainment, setting up clinics on proper maintenance of Airstreams, printing a makeshift newspaper, stringing outside lights. Between the caravans and the rallies, Airstreamers keep busy. They also have the satisfaction of *using* their expensive RVs instead of watching them rust in the driveway. And that, perhaps more than anything else, sells Airstreams.

Each Fourth of July (Wally Byam's birthday!) the huge, week-long International Airstream Rally is held. Fifteen thousand people from all over America converge in their shiny Airstreams on a vacant field in a rural location where they create a comfortable Woodstock for the elderly. Within hours, a city on wheels has been set up and is humming with activity. The Airstream company provides logistical and organizational support, but the international rally is presided over by that year's president, a man who has been able to devote his time for thirteen years to working his way up through lesser Airstream offices, beginning in his local chapter and continuing through ascending regional and then national positions. Airstream has a bewildering array of officers, each of whom is entitled to special insignias, banners, and flags. At the international rally, the president is feted and honored, serves as chief judge of the beauty and talent contests, and walks about greeting everyone and serving as master of ceremonies and host. It is his brief moment in the sun. By the same time next year, he will have become the immediate past president and the first vice president will have moved up to take his place.

"By late Friday afternoon, the Airstreams were pulling into the parking lot."

To see what a local unit rally is like, I spent a spring weekend as guest of the Metro Unit of New York, a club of 160 member trailers, with its own officers, newsletter, and monthly rallies. At this rally, held far out on Long Island in the parking lot of what is, in winter, a public ski area, some fifty trailer-families participated.

By late Friday afternoon, the Airstreams were pulling into the parking lot. Communal events began almost at once, including visiting back and forth between trailers, a potluck supper, a flea market, and a talent show. Euland Bickham, then president of the club, sat on the steps of his trailer, flanked by the American flag and the flag of his office, enjoying the comings and goings of the members. "Everyone here has one thing in common," Bickham said. "Airstream. Whatever the troubles in our neighborhood, or in our jobs if we're not retired, once a month we get away from it all at a rally. Everyone looks out for everyone else here. This is like a little town," Bickham added proudly, looking very much like its mayor.

What impressed me about the people at the rally was their devotion to Airstream and to their club. These people would sooner change their faces as buy a different recreation vehicle, and the club seemed to be one of the most meaningful aspects of their lives. I interviewed members as to why they have Airstreams and are in the club, and this is what they said:

First interviewee: "I bought an Airstream after I visited someone at a rally. I saw how much fun they were having in the club. Being retired I could see that Airstream would give me as many friends as I could want. I *belong* to something now."

Second interviewee: "What I like about Airstreams is that they're all about the same, so you can't tell who's rich or poor in the club."

Third interviewee: "You can *have* camping in tents. You put on a light and everyone can see you from outside. I wanted privacy—and my own toilet. Not to mention air conditioning. This Airstream is my second home—on the road *and* in my driveway. Sometimes when guests come I put them up in the trailer."

Fourth interviewee: "I may be spoiled, but when I travel I want my own bed, my own kitchen, my own everything. Three weeks eating in restaurants would kill me. When I'm in my Airstream, I'm at home while traveling. Not to mention the club: aren't these people beautiful?"

Fifth interviewee: "I bought an Airstream because it was the only trailer that looked like it wasn't going to rattle itself apart. Also, Airstreams drive straight: every other trailer fishtails all over the road. But why am I telling you this baloney? The main reason I have an Airstream is this club: the nicest people I've ever met."

Airstream's success with its club has spawned many imitators. There are clubs for people who have a particular kind of recreation vehicle—motor homes, vans, pickup campers—and clubs for people who subscribe to a particular RV magazine. There are even clubs for RV owners who are also members of a particular fraternal order, such as the Elks, Moose, or Foresters. Since RV people are always looking for an excuse to jump into their RV and go somewhere, the fact that club rallies may be held anywhere in the United States never seems to deter large attendance.

Edith Lane, who writes a regular column in *Trailer Life* magazine called "Lady Alone," founded a club several years ago called Loners on Wheels for single, divorced, or widowed RVers. By now there are over 1500 members and chapters in every state. Lane points out that in the RV world as elsewhere, "being the only single person among a crowd of married couples going two-by-two as in Noah's Ark . . . can only make the single person feel more lonely and lost than if he were entirely alone! We are NOT a 'swinging singles' group," she hastens to add, "but a respectable and respected club, with high standards of behavior which we DO enforce! Our membership is made up of men and women of all ages (though over 70% are of retirement age) and from all walks of life, using all types of RecVees. . . . Many of our members live full-time in their rigs."

Most of the major recreation vehicle manufacturers, in imitation of Airstream, now have their own clubs. Such clubs validate the purchase of an expensive RV by surrounding the owner with a community of like-minded people. "OUR INITIATION FEES START AT $25,000" announces an advertisement for the Sportscoach Owners Club that shows a long line of motor homes traveling together down the highway. "There are two things you must have before you can get in: a Sportscoach; and the heart of a gypsy." As further inducement to buying a Sportscoach, the advertisement continues:

> Just take a look at how our members get around the country in a typical year. Like as not, you'll find them in Miami in January. In Vegas and Lake Havasu in March. And in May they'll be tasting wine and catching trout in the Lake Berryessa-Napa Valley region. Come spring, they're usually up in the Rockies. July probably means Canada and the Great Pacific Northwest. In autumn, it's the changing of the colors in New England. November, when the skies are clear, there's the National Rally in Southern California. Now we ask you, does that sound like our people leave their Sportscoaches parked in their driveways?

The advertisement shows how other manufacturers have learned from Airstream that product loyalty is as much inspired by the total life-style offered as by the quality of the product itself.

Airstream has also been imitated by a number of companies that organize far-flung rallies at such places and events as the Calgary Stampede, Mardi Gras, and Opryland for RVers unassociated with a particular club. Other companies organize overseas caravan tours or combined drive/piggyback train caravans. A variant of the piggyback idea is "camp-a-float," where flat, motorized boats are rented to RVers for travel on lakes and other waterways, the RV becoming an amphibious houseboat whose cabin goes ashore.

Still, no one connected with the RV industry quite provides the service and the sense of *belonging* that Airstream does—or does so with as much élan. Airstream remains the class of the RV industry. This is so largely because of the legacy of Wally Byam. Airstreamers wear his beret and evoke his name at every opportunity. The club and caravans and rallies all carry his name. There is a Wally Byam Foundation in Washington, and the company deposits $10 in the fund for every Airstream purchased. Company, dealers, and Airstream owners alike regularly quote him chapter and verse. If the recreation vehicle industry can be said to have had a prophet, it was Wally Byam.

Chapter IV
Roughing It

An Airstream really isn't camping; it's parking.
Tʜɪs *is camping.*

A pickup camper owner

In his book *Trailer Travel Here and Abroad,* Wally Byam says: "The travel trailer of the future is . . . likely to be an integrated unit, designed so that the small, light, but powerful towing vehicle becomes detachable for use as a pleasure car when you come to a city." Such a recreation vehicle has yet to be built.

Partly this is because recreation vehicles address competitive needs—travel and lodging. Most Americans want an RV to handle both equally well, especially if they can afford only one family vehicle, which is used for transportation during the work week and recreation on weekends. The energy crisis has complicated the problem even more: how do you reduce the fuel consumption of the RV's vehicle portion without sacrificing the comfort of its home portion? The industry is handicapped because half of the RV is manufactured in Detroit, half in Elkhart, and Elkhart hasn't much say about what Detroit produces for it. If the RV industry continues to grow, it might be in a better position to call the shots on what Detroit manufactures. The wheels would be specifically *designed* for the home, and then maybe we would have RVs like the one Wally Byam envisioned.

The closest thing the industry has developed thus far is the pickup camper, half pickup truck, half home. The home part fits into the bed of the truck and hangs over the back. The pickup camper is the recreation vehicle John Steinbeck used when he went about the country gathering material for *Travels with Charlie:*

> I had to go alone and I had to be self-contained, a kind of casual turtle carrying his house on his back. . . . I wanted a three-quarter-ton pick-up truck, capable of going anywhere under possibly rigorous conditions, and on this truck I wanted a little house built like the cabin of a small boat. A trailer is difficult to maneuver on mountain roads, is impossible and often illegal to park, and is subject to many restrictions. In due time, specifications came through for a tough, fast,

comfortable vehicle, mounting a camper top—a little house with double bed, a four-burner stove, a heater, refrigerator and lights operating on butane, a chemical toilet, closet space, storage space, windows screened against insects—exactly what I wanted. . . . It arrived in August, a beautiful thing, powerful and yet lithe. It was almost as easy to handle as a passenger car.

The way a pickup camper works is like this. The home, or camper portion, raises up on stilt-like jacks. (You've probably seen these strange architectural forms in driveways and yards all over America without knowing what they were.) With the camper standing there raised up, the pickup is backed under it. Then the jacks are lowered, the camper is settled down into the truck bed, and the pickup camper is ready to roll. It's as easy as that. To dismount the camper, you reverse the process: the camper is raised out of the truck bed on its stilt-like jacks, and the pickup is driven out from under it.

While the two parts of pickup campers are not as easily separable as Wally Byam hoped, they're sufficiently so that, with a little work, the RVer can have an unencumbered pickup truck at his disposal. This is a tremendous advantage—especially to those who already own a pickup or are thinking of buying one. So people into pickup camping usually have an affinity for pickups or are at least familiar with them. Many use them regularly in their work—in the construction trades, farming, etc. Usually people who own pickup campers live in rural or semi-rural areas where there is enough room to set up the camper when it is dismounted.

People who own pickup campers are often blue-collar outdoorsmen heavily into fishing and hunting and above luxury. The Airstream, the "Cadillac" of recreation vehicles, is anathema to them. They would sooner go for the "Jeep."

Coachmen Industries of Middlebury, Indiana, just down the road from Elkhart, is the number one manufacturer of pickup campers. They did a survey of their clientele a few years back that included this profile of purchasers of pickup campers:

—— Middle-aged, working-class man with average income and below average education. He tends to be dissatisfied with current job, yet has few options. He works with his hands and is proud of his skills.

—— Interests are outdoor activities and adventure
—Hunting, fishing, camping
—He enjoys the outdoors
—Fantasy adventure and action

—— He can pursue these interests, as he tends to live in rural areas. Over half live outside metropolitan areas. Little interest in the city and no plans to move.

—— Feels in debt and wishes for money to take care of his needs and needs of large family. Yet he does little to control debt.
—Impulse orientation
—Poor planner
—Needs discipline imposed from outside

—— Except for outdoor activities, he is a homebody. Not active socially, in organizations, or in his community.

—— Traditional and closed minded in attitudes
—Male-female role
—Social change is frightening
—Skeptical of big business and government

—— Because of low education and rural orientation, cultural experiences have little meaning to him.
—Doesn't read
—Prefers entertainment on TV
—No interest in art, music, or theater
—Media preferences are centered around his outdoor interests and adventure orientation.

—— In his television preferences he is especially interested in traditional, male action and outdoor-nature programs. This is prevalent in his above-average preference for:

Man from Shiloh	Gunsmoke
ABC Wide World of Sports	Bonanza
Major League Baseball	F.B.I.
Medical Center	World of Disney
Marcus Welby	Network Movies

—— These same preferences run through the few magazines that he reads:

Field and Stream	Argosy
Popular Mechanics	True
Farm Journal	TV Guide

One of my neighbors, David Hodgkins, has a pickup camper and fits the Coachmen profile. He's a high school graduate, works in a factory, and subscribes to *Popular Mechanics* and *Field and Stream.* All the kids in the neighborhood like to hang out near David's camper, but the adults regard it as slightly weird because they all drive sedans and have middle-class values into which pickup trucks don't fit, and pickup campers even less. It may be that envy is part of their attitude: every weekend David and his wife head for the Jersey shore in their pickup camper to camp out in the dunes and fish in the surf.

Pickup campers are built rugged so they can go into areas no automobile or other RV can handle. If the pickup has four-wheel drive, it can go almost anywhere—along beaches, up mountains, wherever. That's why Jack Sanders bought a pickup camper. Sanders is a retired Maine construction worker who used pickups all his working life. A few years ago, he bought himself a new Chevrolet pickup and then a Mapleleaf Camper to fit it. Sanders likes to travel into the backwoods where he's been spending summers building a cabin while living in his pickup camper. He drives it in there along an old logging trail. He spends the better part of the spring and fall living in his mobile home, but, in summer, heads for the woods in the camper.

To avoid the Maine winter, Sanders goes down to Florida in the pickup camper. It has a refrigerator, stove, chemical toilet, holding tanks for water and sewage, a dining area, can convert to

A homemade pickup camper.

sleep five (sometimes he takes his grandchildren along)—yet the camper weighs only 1405 pounds, and Sanders gets twelve miles per gallon on the road with it in place.

In Florida, Sanders usually looks for a nice campground. He dismounts the camper from the pickup and puts it on cement blocks—which are safer than jacks in high winds, not to mention Florida hurricanes. He switches off the 12-volt electrical system connected to the pickup's two batteries and hooks the camper up to the campground's 110-volt current so he can run his lights all he wants and plug in his Sony color TV. He hooks up the camper's water system to the campground's supply with a garden hose and then has water under pressure without having to refill his tank or use his water pump. Finally, he connects his sewage drain to the concrete cesspool, giving him an automatic toilet. (When he's on the road, he has to stop every few days at a campground or gas station dump facility. Usually they charge him a buck to dump his sewage, though there are gas stations that let you dump for free if you fill up or have some mechanical work done there.)

Once Sanders has his camper set up at the campsite, he's free to drive around in the pickup all winter without it costing gas to lug the camper around. The camper being there gives him a sense of going home each time he returns to the campground. He admits it's "silly" but Sanders sometimes enjoys heading back to his camper instead of its being "on my back"—though, other times, he likes traveling with it and having "that nice feeling that I can stop anytime, anywhere, climb in the back, lock the door, and go to sleep."

Sanders seems perfectly delighted with his life in retirement, especially his independence: "I feel just like a kid," he says. "I don't know why people put all that money into regular houses. They must be crazy. Do you realize that for what a stickbuilt house would cost me I have the mobile home, the pickup camper, my land in the woods, and plenty of money left over to build the cabin. If I had a stickbuilt house that's *all* I would have; I'd be moldering away on a rocking chair right now. Hey, and let's not forget: I have the pickup truck, my transportation, as part of the deal."

When you look at a pickup truck, you realize it was almost made to be a recreation vehicle. The bed of the truck was there from the start as a place to sleep, and the first "pickup campers" were just that—pickup trucks people camped out in. Folks did that a lot in the Depression, stretching a piece of canvas across the top of the truck bed to make it a watertight compartment. From there it was a hop, skip, and a jump to someone lowering the tailgate and introducing a wooden structure into the bed— like sliding a drawer into a cupboard or chest.

But it took Walt King, of the Sport King Company of Nampa, Idaho, to come up with the idea for the pickup camper per se. In 1944, King was towing a trailer behind his pickup truck on a hunting trip in the Northwest when he was caught in an early snowstorm. He had to leave the trailer behind, and the only way he could get his pickup going was to fill the truck bed with rocks for traction. Later, it occurred to him: "Why not mount a trailer body right on the pickup truck?" It would provide traction, would be far more maneuverable than a trailer, and it wouldn't be much heavier than the rocks he had hauled. The next year, King designed a pickup camper for himself and went off on his vacation in it, not knowing that he had actually invented something. While stopped by the road in Montana, a sheepherder came galloping up to see the strange-looking vehicle. "I'll take five of them," he said. "Five of what?" King asked, incredulous. The sheepherder peeled off five one hundred dollar bills as a deposit, and an industry was born.

The pickup camper is the easiest RV to manufacture, because there are no moving parts; it doesn't even have its own wheels. The cratelike camper shell is hammered together by a carpenter; it's insulated and aluminum siding is put on; and furniture and appliances are installed. That's it. It's so easy, hundreds of companies make them, and they are forever going in and out of business.

Some pickup camper units have a canvas section that expands

outward on the side or back when parked, providing an extra miniroom with a double bed. Sleeping in it or the other spaces of a pickup camper is kind of tight, but comfortable enough once everyone is tucked away. It's a little like berths in the old-style Pullmans. If RV manufacturers do one thing well, it's making use of space ingeniously. Whether or not RVs are antienvironment (as some think), pickup camper life is on such a simple scale it should gladden the heart of the most uncompromising ecologist.

Most pickup campers have a cabover section with a double bed in it, which makes them look like mini motor homes. But there is a basic difference. In the motor home, the chassis and home are welded together, so there's no dismounting the home as with the pickup camper. Also, with the motor home, you can walk from the cab back into the home, while with a pickup camper, you have to get out of the truck and go around to the back door of the home to get inside.

This can be a crucial difference—in communication as well as in convenience. A story every RVer knows is about the man who was 150 miles down the road from his last campsite when a state policeman pulled up behind him with siren screaming and lights flashing. The man assumed he was about to get a speeding ticket, and was preparing his defense, when the trooper walked up to his window and asked if he was Harold Crosby. Not knowing how the trooper could possibly know his name unless he was guilty of something even more serious than speeding, the man stammered "Yyyyyyesss." The trooper said he had received a Missing Persons radio bulletin on Crosby placed by his wife. "That's silly," said Crosby, "my wife is asleep in the back." "Show me," the state trooper said. So Crosby got out of the cab, went around to the back of the pickup camper, opened the door and—*Voilà!* No wife. When he completed the three-hundred-mile round trip, Crosby found his wife calmly playing cards with the people at the next campsite. "Have a nice time dear?" she asked.

Another story concerns a man who rose in the middle of the night in his pickup camper to urinate in the bushes and stepped outside on the highway at 50 MPH, unaware, in his somnolent state, that his restless son had awakened some time before and decided to push on for a few hours. Maybe it was because he was almost asleep that the man bounced off the road uninjured except for some scratches, but he had difficulty explaining to the police in the next town what he was doing walking around in the middle of the night in his underwear, and it took two days before he and his son were reunited. I might mention that, to avoid some of these problems, intercom systems between truck and home are becoming big sellers for pickup campers, and there is even a pickup camper being manufactured now that provides a crawl-through space between the pickup and the camper.

Had such a pickup camper existed some years ago, it might have saved one man a great deal of trouble. Art Rouse, of *Trailer Life* magazine, tells the story:

> The wife of a cocktail bar owner, suspicious that her husband was using the family pickup camper as the vehicle for his extramarital affair with one of the barmaids, hid in the shadows of the parking lot one night after closing. When the amorous couple emerged from the bar and entered the coach, the irate wife started the truck's engine and took off in a cloud of dust, spending the next two or three hours driving over the roughest, bumpiest roads she could find. Arriving home, she backed the camper firmly up against the garage and went inside the house to bed. Arising early the next morning, she telephoned the police, a photographer, and a lawyer. When they arrived, she led them out to the driveway, moved the camper away from the garage, and allowed the illicit lovers to emerge amid the glare of exploding flashbulbs!

Related to the pickup camper as an RV is the kap, a fiberglass cover for the truck bed which gives the pickup a sedan look. A kap can cost as little as $200, depending on whether it has windows and a door and how high it is. Some people with

A stack of kaps.

pickups buy themselves a kap and then, after a while, build a little home inside, laying a floor and paneling and insulating the sides of the truck bed. Then they bring in furniture, kitchen sinks—whatever. When you get up to that kind of kapped pickup it's hard to say whether you have a kap or a pickup camper—maybe a little of both.

Though the pickup camper and pickup with kap are the primary RVs for roughing it on the road, some people go so far as to turn their automobiles into homes. Sue and Joe Alcorn, of Bedford, Massachusetts, lived in their 1965 Ford LTD station wagon for a year. They took out the back seat and laid a double bed mattress in there. They put curtains on the back and side windows which they drew at night. Then they mounted a little wooden cupboard for food, a one-burner Coleman propane stove, and a tiny refrigerator, which also runs on propane, against the front seat of the car.

When Sue and Joe graduated from college, they took off to live on the road for a while before deciding what they wanted to do professionally and where they wanted to settle. They spent the fall and winter months in the Sun Belt states, cruising from Southern California and Mexico around to Florida, and spent the spring and summer months in the North—Michigan, Montana, British Columbia.

Sue and Joe found they could make out on as little as $3 a day for food for the two of them! Rent was free, and their only big expense was gas. They used bathrooms in gas stations and bathed in rivers and lakes. The whole year cost them a little over $3000, and they were able to pick most of this up doing odd jobs along the way. Neither one of them had a cold the whole year. In fact, Joe's allergies mysteriously disappeared. Most important in a country where everyone seems to be increasingly terrified of everyone else, they were never once bothered by anyone during the year—no thieves, no murderers, no rapists. The only people who ever molested them were the police, who assumed that since they were living in their car they must be up to no good and made them move on. Except for the cops, Sue and Joe enjoyed the year so much that, toward the end of it, which is when I met them, they were agonizing over whether to settle down or keep doing what they were doing. "At the very least," Joe said, "we're going to do this again a few years from now."

Inspired by the Alcorns, I took off for a New England weekend and lived in my Volvo. Though a foreign car seems on the opposite end of the automotive spectrum from an RV, the back seat of the Volvo station wagon folds flat and then you have a space in there eight feet long by almost four feet wide. What I liked best was lying in the back and looking up at the dashboard and steering wheel, knowing that any time I felt like it I could get up and drive. One of the two nights I was out, I awoke at two o'clock for some reason and thought, "Wouldn't it be fine to just drive along in the dark down these country roads—never mind that this is when you're supposed to be sleeping?" I did just that—drove along till four, when I stopped in a diner for something to eat and discovered this whole wideawake world of truckers and night-shift people and country music blaring like all Nashville. Afterwards, I found a roadside rest stop by a beach and pulled in and went back to sleep, awaking later to the sound of the ocean.

There never was a time when I felt so affectionately toward my car—in tune with it, the road, nature. It was, after all, my wheels *and* my home, and what else does a man require? For once there were no rules except the ones I made; like Thoreau at Walden, I lived deliberately, purposefully—even if only for two days. I also felt like a kid—playing. The experience reminded me somehow of Robert Louis Stevenson's poem about the children who build a "boat" out of chairs on the upstairs landing and sail away to a make-believe world.

That's probably how Marshall and Helen Greason feel some of the time. They live in their Ford Club Wagon, which they've converted into a permanent home on wheels by installing a 2 cubic-foot refrigerator, a closet, a two burner LP stove, a sink, a dining nook that magically changes at night into their 70 x 54 inch bed, and a storage area on the roof, where they also tote a kayak. And the Greasons are in their sixties, retired—not some young kids. They like living in a small rig with such a spartan setup. "Ease of travel," is the reason Helen gives:

> When we first started out six years ago, after Marshall retired, our oldest son insisted we use their 30-foot Airstream on our first trip. We had sold our house not long before, a big one with four bedrooms and lots of yard. It was a brute to keep up. Their Airstream was certainly luxurious and plenty big for the two of us. It had two drawbacks, though, as far as I was concerned. It was just too big to keep clean and was just loaded with sophisticated gadgets. I found I was spending too much time just keeping house. That wasn't what I had in mind for our retirement.

"We don't have a real home anymore," Helen Greason adds. "Oh we can stay for a few weeks anytime with one of our kids back East. They have good-sized homes and we're always welcome. But this is what we live in now." Perhaps they can enjoy life in such confined quarters because they basically *live out of,* rather than in, their camper, and because both Marshall and Helen practice yoga regularly. They also are vegetarians—so they do not have to store meat, and most of their food does not require refrigeration. "We just eat what's in season wherever we go," says Marshall. In a space not much bigger, if that, than the bathrooms in many of our homes, the Greasons are living full-time on the road, traveling to Alaska in summer, to Mexico in winter, following up their hobby of bird-watching, spreading their yoga mats every morning in the sun to do their exercises—doing what they feel like when they feel like it.

There are a couple of products on the market now for people who wish to live out of their automobiles but need to expand their space when they settle for the night. American Motors sells a gadget that fits into its hatchback models and blooms outward from the trunk to become a tent when the car is stationary. It's similar to the apparatus sold by Ford early in the century that unfolded from the side of the Model T to become a tent.

There is also a device called the Jutter which attaches to the roofs of vans and large station wagons and converts, in two minutes, into a double bed loft plus an 8 x 8 side room at ground level. Styled as "The Instant RV," the Jutter was designed by an architect with a love for travel and camping but little patience for setting up and taking down a tent every night, not enough room in his van to sleep his family comfortably, and no desire to tow a tent trailer.

However, a tent trailer worked perfectly for the Blickley family of Grand Rapids, Michigan, a few years ago when they embarked on a two thousand mile trek across the Sahara Desert from Algeria to Nigeria. William Blickley, his wife La Verne, and their sons Eric and Adam traveled in a Jeep Wagoneer and towed a Jayco tent trailer as their home. The trip began in a beautiful campground in Algiers and ended beside a lovely country club in Kano, Nigeria. In between was a largely trackless wilderness, full of danger and death, more appropriate to camels than to a recreation vehicle.

The tent trailer was ideal for the Blickleys, since it is light weight, easy to tow, and more open to the air than other RVs. It is, therefore, a favorite, along with the pickup camper, of RVers interested in roughing it. If the pickup camper tends to be the RV of choice for blue-collar America, the tent trailer tends to be the RV of choice for young, middle class families who like camping but no longer want to tent. Most owners of tent trailers previously were tenters.

As mentioned earlier, the tent trailer was probably the first RV. It developed when Model T owners, tired of sleeping on the ground in tents, began to cart them along on flatbed trailers. Soon they were being manufactured, and they sold well because they were convenient and inexpensive. However, as more and more sophisticated RVs came along, tent trailers, which were considered primitive (midway, really, between a tent and a trailer), declined in sales—this tendency continuing until the

energy crunch reversed it. With the downsizing of cars and
engines and the concern for fuel economy, tent trailers have
again become popular sellers. There are tent trailers which, fully
equipped, weigh as little as nine hundred pounds. Also, once
folded down, tent trailers are so compact they are usually lower
than the vehicle pulling them—so there is little wind resistance
and little increase in fuel consumption over what the towing
vehicle alone uses. Coleman, a leading manufacturer of tent
trailers, uses the advertising slogans "More Fun Per Gallon!" and
"100 Miles Per Gallon"—meaning that it takes only one extra
gallon of gas to tow its tent trailer a hundred miles.

Although tent trailers are for RVers who see themselves as
only one step removed from tenting, more luxury features are
added to them every year: fold out mini rooms, propane-
powered stoves and refrigerators, dinettes, toilets, water and
sewage tanks, electric lights. The RV industry is always coming
up with ingenious gadgets to make RVs more luxurious—
requiring the "reinvention" of more humble RVs to fill the needs
of those who see themselves basically as campers.

Camping is an enormous growth industry in the United
States—for tenters and also, increasingly, for RVers. In many
campgrounds these days, one hardly sees a tent, so covered is
the landscape with RVs of all kinds. In 1976, the last year for
which statistics are available, there were a total of 8,166 privately
owned campgrounds in the United States and 4,655 publicly
owned campgrounds, with well over a million individual sites
between them. KOA, the largest of the privately owned
campground chains, is a major corporation that sells stock and
has close to nine hundred campgrounds scattered throughout all
fifty states, Canada, and Mexico. It began operations as recently
as 1962, with one campground in Billings, Montana, where its
executive offices are now located. The McDonalds of the
campground business, KOA provides swimming pools, stores,
community centers, and organized activities such as square
dancing at its campgrounds. KOA also rents tents and RVs.

In recent years, major motel chains, such as Holiday Inn and

Ramada Inn, have gotten into the campground industry as a sideline—especially in scenic areas where people prefer camping out-of-doors to staying in a motel. With the fashionable ecology, physical fitness, and do-it-yourself movements, motels find themselves increasingly competing with campgrounds for customers. A story in the *Colorado Springs Sun* in the summer of 1978 is headlined "RVs, Campers, Blamed in Motel-Rental Decline."

Disneyland in California and Disney World in Florida are the places to really see campgrounds and motels competing with one another. There, RV cities sprawl over hundreds of acres on the outskirts of which are motels. As a cantankerous gentleman from Tennessee said to me at Disneyland while sitting on the back stoop of his pickup camper savoring a beer, "Hell, why should I stay over there in them motels? I've got my *own* motel right here!"

Chapter V
Mobile Mansions

Who Says "When You Leave Home, You Can't Take It With You?"

advertisement by a motor home manufacturer

T*ime* magazine reports:

The Winnebago lurking on the shore of Chesapeake Bay one recent weekend looked like any other mobile camper, but with the radio scanner and communication equipment inside, it resembled a war room in the Pentagon. As a command post for the onshore operations of a marijuana smuggling confederacy, it had been monitoring the area's police for a week, preparing for a mother ship's arrival in nearby waters. The camper was in contact with small trucks and vans waiting along the coast for the merchandise. As the ship reached the southern tip of Assateague Island, five miles off Virginia, the camper, using code that would bewilder a CB buff, arranged meetings with the contact speedboats and guided them back to rendezvous points on the shore.

An unusual use for a motor home? Yes, but not unique. The ultimate in homes on wheels, the motor home can be used for virtually anything. Dr. W. B. Chastain, of Modesto, California, has a motor home equipped for home obstetrics. When an expectant mother in labor phones him, he drives to her house, parks in the driveway, checks her out, and returns to his motor home to await developments. There he sleeps or watches television, or otherwise relaxes, ready at an instant's notice. He delivers the baby in the patient's own bed, in familiar surroundings. If there are complications, he has sophisticated backup equipment in the motor home.

Motor homes have been used as mobile offices, as mobile display rooms for wholesale or retail sales ("If you can't get the customer to the store, bring the store to the customer" is the motto of several Minolta copier salesmen who use motor homes installed with copiers and the generators to run them), as mobile libraries and classrooms, as mobile hearing and speech therapy clinics, as mobile beauty parlors for rural areas, and as mobile headquarters for political candidates. Foreign potentates like the King of Saudi Arabia have used specially commissioned motor homes as air conditioned mobile throne rooms to hold court in outlying districts. The author, Carla Emery, used a motor home to tour ninety-three cities in the United States promoting a book. Jean Shepherd used a motor home to travel about the country when he produced his television series "Jean Shepherd's America." Finally, a recent advertisement in the "Personals" section of *The Village Voice* newspaper in New York further illustrates the range of the motor home's appeal: "MAN, 49, seeks Female companion to tour U.S. in motor home. Non-smoker pref. Box 464, Tuckerton, N.J. 08087."

Motor homes are the most sophisticated of recreation vehicles in terms of their flexibility and self-containment. They combine the luxury of the large trailer with the portability of the pickup camper. In addition, since the driving compartment and home are one integrated unit, cooking, eating, washing dishes or clothes, cleaning, sleeping, making beds, making love, playing games of all sorts, using the toilet, showering—in short, virtually anything domestic—may be done while underway. When a family parks for the night, it is already settled. Dinner may have been prepared while on the road and be on the table. Beds are ready to crawl into. No one need go outside unless he desires to. In the morning the family can be underway as soon as the driver is out of bed, even while the others are still sleeping.

A motor home is the ultimate in mobility, togetherness, and security—a combination vacation home and mobile fortress. Sportscoach Motor Homes regularly publishes a two-page advertisement which shows a mansion on one page with the notation "SPORTSCOACH AS SEEN BY OUR INTERIOR DESIGNERS" and a military tank on the other page with the notation "SPORTSCOACH AS SEEN BY OUR ENGINEERS."

A motor home is ideal for families. I rented a twenty-foot Winnebago Minnie Winnie one Christmas vacation and took my sons to the Florida Keys in it for a week. We got to the Keys from New Jersey in less than a day, my sons and I spelling each other on the driving. Except for gas, we never stopped. Those of us not driving slept, read, or played chess. The propane heater kept us warm on the way south, the fiberglass bathroom compartment was adequate as long as the driver made no sudden stops, and the cabinets and refrigerator were stocked with food. We often made popcorn while underway—the vertical explosions of the popping corn contrasting with our smooth, horizontal progress.

Given the size of the Winnebago, and the many hours of uninterrupted travel, the trip down to the Keys was more like a transoceanic airplane flight than an automobile ride. When we finally emerged from the motor home we experienced a disorientation not unlike jet lag. It was as if we hadn't been on the road, but watching a movie of what went by outside. My son David put it another way: "It feels like there's really four of us on this trip, Dad: you, me, Jeffrey, and the Winnebago."

During our seven nights on the road we spent a fortune on gasoline but virtually nothing on lodging. I was forever miserable watching our gas gauge descend but cheered up each night as we bedded down. Two nights (down and back) we drove straight through; one night we stopped in a school parking lot in the Keys; one night in a gas station where we had filled our tank; one night in a roadside rest stop; New Year's Eve in the Key West municipal parking lot at the very end of U.S. 1 (returning to the motor home to sleep after half a night of carousing about the streets). The only night we paid anything for was in Key West when we pulled into a drive-in movie at midnight just after the show ended. The owner charged us the same "$3 a carload" to spend the night as he had charged for the show. We pulled in next to the darkened concrete screen, parting waves of candy wrappers and soft drink containers, and instantly went to sleep.

Besides their appeal to families, motor homes find a strong market among the elderly. The Boone sisters, of Calais, Maine, are direct descendants of Daniel Boone and, like their famous ancestor, have a lot of restless energy. Daniel Boone moved on whenever he could see smoke from the next man's chimney fire. He craved his own land, his own forest. Similarly, the Boone sisters spend three months each year traveling in their Dodge

Travco motor home. Mary and Florence are retired schoolteachers, and Ethel is a retired department store manager. Though all three women are in their seventies, they have already traveled three times to Alaska from Maine.

Proving that elderly women motor homers can also travel alone, Peggy Hoskins, a widow from Morton Grove, Illinois, whose children are grown, sold her ten-room house several years ago when she was sixty-two and embarked on a full-time life on the road in a newly purchased Winnebago. She had never driven anything but an automobile before but soon learned there is nothing different about driving a motor home as long as you allow for its greater size. Mrs. Hoskins refers to herself as "a turtle" because, like that animal, "I carry my home on my back."

Probably the most intrepid motor homer on the road in recent years has been Walter Casey Jones, of Tacoma, Washington. At the age of 103, the white-bearded Jones, who is often mistaken for Colonel Sanders, bought a motor home and took off on a solo two-year tour of the United States. Having lived through the administrations of twenty-two presidents and started up a new business at age ninety-two, Jones found time on his hands after his wife of fifty-two years died. He followed through on a longtime dream, bought himself a motor home, and hit the road. After a serious heart attack in 1959, Jones had been told by his doctors that he would spend the rest of his life in a wheel chair. "I sure fooled them," he says.

One reason motor homes are ideal for travel by the elderly is because much of the trauma of traveling is eliminated. Those on diets and medication can readily take care of themselves. They prepare their own meals and have their own beds to sleep in every night. Whatever their adventures, their domestic life remains reassuringly constant and comfortable, even luxurious.

The luxury of motor homes suggested to me several titles for this chapter, such as "Land Yachts" and "Palaces on Wheels." I finally decided on "Mobile Mansions" after coming across a Snuffy Smith comic strip in the Sunday papers. In the strip, Snuffy the hillbilly is visiting a friend who, clad like an aristocrat in a smoking jacket, is showing Snuffy around what appears to be a huge and elegant mansion. Snuffy is shown past a central courtyard with fountain, a den, a modern, fully equipped kitchen, an indoor swimming pool. But in the last drawing, when Snuffy departs, *he* says "Drap by ag'in." To which his friend replies "Next vacation time for sure, Snuffy." Only then does the reader notice that the friend has been showing Snuffy around his motor home.

Caricaturing motor homes is not new. In 1910, an artist made fun of what must have been the first motor home by drawing it with a swimming pool and tennis court on the roof. The motor home was commissioned by Mr. U. H. Dandurand, a wealthy real estate agent in Montreal, for family weekend outings. Built on a three-ton Packard truck chassis, the body was an adaptation of the Pullman train car design of the times and slept thirteen. The Dandurands traveled with a chauffeur and a footman, whose jobs included cranking the motor, getting frightened horses out of the way, and reinforcing doubtful bridges. When it was retired from the road many years later, the Dandurand's motor home was turned into a summer cottage.

By the 1920s, a number of people were commissioning or building what were then called "house cars." Ira Flanagan and Marvin Mann, who lived in Buchanan, Michigan, decided to go West to seek their fortunes. "We both liked to tinker with autos," Flanagan relates, "and it was natural that we decided to make a home on wheels." "Actually," says Mann, "we took a new Ford one-and-a-half-ton Model T truck and built a tar paper shack around it." Despite its primitive nature, the Flanagan-Mann motor home included such comforts as running water from a thirty-gallon tank, a sink, a two burner Coleman gasoline stove, a built-in bookcase, two bunks, and a wardrobe. Flanagan and Mann's only difficulty with their motor home was that it was topheavy and always in danger of turning over on the primitive roads of those days. Going through the Rockies, one drove while the other pushed off against the mountainside with a long pole to keep the motor home upright.

In 1924, Ford manufactured what it called a "camping car," with some properties of a motor home. It was built on a one-ton truck chassis and had a body of sheet steel fastened to hardwood supports and a roof of rubberized fabric. The unit came with a choice of double bed or bunk beds but offered little else. Basically, it was the shell of a motor home. Buyers improvised from there.

The man credited with mass producing the first motor home—a self-contained unit with all the amenities—was Ray Frank. In 1958, Frank built such a travel vehicle for his family and coined the word "motor home" to describe it. So much interest was expressed in it when he took it on the road, that a year or so later, Frank was manufacturing units similar to his own in a barn near Brown City, Michigan. He built six units in 1960 and jumped to 131 the following year. In 1963 he introduced an all-fiberglass body. Indicative of how new the motor home industry is, Frank—often called "the father of motor homes"—is the still youthful chairman of the board of Frank Industries, which is still located in Brown City, Michigan.

Another indication of the newness of the motor home industry is that when Wally Byam wrote his book *Trailer Travel Here and Abroad* (1960), he referred to motor homes with the antique term "house cars." Wally, always the trailerist, wasn't keen on motor homes. He opined that they might be useful "on expeditions to the less developed parts of the world . . . like a tank or snowmobile," but he found them too big and too expensive. "Such vehicles can never be more than miniature Greyhound buses," he wrote.

Despite Wally's doubts, *House Beautiful* magazine did a twelve-page cover story only four years later called "Meet The Land Yachts: A New Breed of Rolling Home." Said the magazine, "A new kind of vehicle has been born while you were not looking. It is a cross between a bus and a travel-trailer, and superior to both." *House Beautiful* also evaluated eleven makes of motor homes being manufactured by 1964.

Since 1964, motor home production has exploded, taking over

"The industry has been responding to the fuel crisis by building smaller and smaller motor homes."

an increasing proportion of total recreation vehicle sales. The greatest inroad in recent years has been made by mini motor homes, and the biggest sufferer has been pickup campers, which they resemble. In 1977, 119,000 motor homes were sold as compared with 9,000 a decade before. Were it not for concern over fuel, motor homes would probably dominate the RV industry by now.

The industry has been responding to the fuel crisis by building smaller and smaller motor homes. While some of the large motor homes are still thirty-five and even forty feet long, get as little as three to four miles per gallon, and cost $40,000, there are tiny motor homes today which get better mileage than many automobiles. Basically, motor homes break down into three categories: Class A motor homes, which are built on a truck chassis and usually are twenty-three feet or longer; mini motor homes, which have the same cabover configuration as a pickup camper, are built on a modified van chassis, and are usually from seventeen to twenty-three feet long; and the latest entries into the market, micro-minis, which are shorter than seventeen feet and built on Toyota and Datsun chassis.

Class A motor homes are rarely seen these days without bicycles or motorcycles strapped to their bumpers. Many tow small automobiles so that the motor home itself does not have to be used for travel in and around a destination point. Some of the smaller motor homes, despite their bulk, are actually shorter than station wagons, and the sales pitch for them often compares the two. "What station wagon can offer you sleeping quarters for four, a bathroom, water storage and bottled gas, and a full kitchen?" asks an advertisement for Casual Mini Motor Homes. However, most mini motor homes get no better than ten miles per gallon, so the micro-minis are increasingly the competitive part of the market. There are micro-minis which get twenty-five miles per gallon on the highway and cost as little as $8,000. "Back to Basics," an advertisement for Mirage Micro-Mini Motor Homes argues. "You've had it with your Goliath Motor Home. All 40 feet of it. With its combination built-in lettuce chopper and early warning frostbite detector. And its five gallons to the mile."

Despite the general downsizing of motor homes, there are still people who crave large and expensive ones. Blue Bird Wanderlodge, a Georgia-based manufacturer of school buses, produces a luxury motor home with the appearance of a bus which ranges in price between $70,000 and $110,000. But the most extraordinary motor homes in America are those created by Newell Coach, in Miami, Oklahoma. Newell builds all its motor homes from scratch to the specifications of the customer, "breaking the assembly-line barrier" as the company puts it. They cost $140,000 and up, but there are enough Americans wealthy enough to purchase just what they want in a motor home to keep Newell busy.

The company which manufactures by far the greatest number of motor homes, and at moderate prices, is, of course, Winnebago. When my sons and I rented a motor home, it never occurred to us to look for anything but a Winnebago—even though there must be a hundred other brands. Winnebago is the only motor home regularly advertised nationally. "A Condominium That Goes Places" is its current slogan. With its familiar flying *W* insignia and cratelike shape, *Winnebago* means "motor home" for most Americans.

The Winnebago company is located in Forest City, Winnebago County, in the corn and hogs country of northern Iowa. The company and county derive their name from the Winnebago Indians who once made their home in the area, and some of Winnebago's models—Indian, Brave, Chieftain—reflect the Indian past.

Winnebago is the largest manufacturer in the state of Iowa, and the Forest City plant, with over fifty acres of manufacturing space under roof, is the largest recreation vehicle complex in the world. But Forest City is a small town, with only 4400 residents—making it necessary for Winnebago to bus in many of its 3500 workers from farms and communities as far as fifty miles away. "We're a little country Iowa operation," John Hanson, company president, likes to say. When I visited Forest City, my car's water pump began breaking down, and it was necessary to drive all the way to Des Moines to get another one or wait two weeks for one to be shipped to Forest City.

Forest City is a company town in every sense of the word. Not only do most residents work at Winnebago; everyone with any spare cash has it invested in the company. The chief sport in town is hanging out at the local office of M. Wittenstein and Co., which posts the price of Winnebago stock in its windows. I talked to a storeowner who told me his stock was worth $200,000 in early 1973 but crashed to $25,000 at the height of the oil embargo of 1973–1974. It crept back up after 1974 but took another dive in 1979. Similarly, Winnebago plummeted from 3500 to 800 employees in 1973–1974. A year later it was up to 2200 and had slowly climbed back to its normal level by 1977. But in 1979, there were massive layoffs once again.

In early 1973, Winnebago had experienced its eighth consecutive year of record sales and earnings and was in the midst of a massive expansion program. It had expected to be running double shifts and producing 1200 motor homes per week soon, and John Hanson had happily pointed out, "The recreation vehicle industry is the fastest growing industry in the country. . . . The opportunities ahead are enormous." Six months later, Winnebago, along with much of the recreation vehicle industry, was crippled. Winnebago was particularly hurt because 90 percent of its production is in motor homes.

The company has tried to diversify somewhat in recent years. It has gone into the motor home rental business ("Rent a Comfortable Home With a View" its advertisements read). It has tried, but without success, to market the Heli-home, a helicopter with some home features aboard. It has built a great number of agricultural trailers, fifth wheels, and kaps. And it has a new Living Components Division, which manufactures prefabricated buildings.

But motor homes is where the company will be made or broken. Recently, Winnebago produced the first American-made

"Your Winnebago can be a beachfront property."

diesel motor home and the first motor home which can run on both gasoline and propane. The company is also stressing the "modular capacity" of its motor home interiors. Buyers are being encouraged to "Be Your Own Interior Designer" by choosing floor layouts ("*You* decide where you want to put the master bedroom, the bath, and the family room"), furniture, appliances, and fabrics. The suggestion is that there can be as much choice in buying and decorating a Winnebago as in buying and decorating a home. One brochure states, "Your Winnebago can be a beachfront property, a mountain retreat, an elegant townhouse, or a fine home in the country." A suggested motor home design has a Victorian interior reminiscent of "the great days of railroading." Another, calling itself "The Sportsmen's Den," is designed to resemble a hunting lodge. A third, calling itself "The Seafarer," includes in its decor a brass-plated ship's clock, a ship's wheel mirror in the bathroom, a brass captain's bell, and a "weather center" with dials for temperature, humidity, and barometric pressure. "A Winnebago is more than a motor home," says the company. "It's a life-style."

While stressing the luxury and homelike qualities of their motor homes, Winnebago isn't forgetting their connections with the frontier past. One brochure reads: "A Great American Said, 'Go West Young Man.' Now It's Possible For Americans, Young And Not So Young, To Head East, West, North And South With The Same Spirit Of The Pioneers And In Their *Own* Covered Wagons." In motor homes, the simultaneous and contradictory American desire to live in a mansion while being completely free and mobile reaches a kind of apotheosis. "This is my home," a Winnebago owner said to me. And then he kicked one of his tires for emphasis.

"along the floor, up the walls, and around the ceiling in one continuous cocoon, the ultimate in wall to wall"

Chapter VI
Rolling Rooms

When This Van's A 'Rockin'
Don't Come A Knockin'
Van bumper sticker

Vantastic is parked away from the others as befits its station. It has eight coats of paint and what isn't painted is a dazzling chrome. The hood is up so you can see that the motor, which is so clean it wouldn't be out of place in an operating room, is chromed, too. Not to mention the plush, velvet-upholstered battery. What gets the most attention, though, is the painting of the beautiful woman—blonde in a black evening gown—stretched out along the length of the van. This is no cheap nude like young vanners go for; this is a *lady,* someone with character. Anyone who takes the trouble to have a painting like this on his van, you can tell he's a serious type.

Still, it's the inside of *Vantastic* that gets you. They say Joe Doherty has $20,000 in this van, and it mainly shows inside. Joe has a bar with cold beer on tap in the living room. Beyond the fancy wrought iron grate is the step-up bedroom. The bedroom has an honest-to-goodness heart-shaped bed across the back of the van, heart-shaped mirrors on the wall, a heart-shaped bedspread, and heart-shaped, stained glass windows. The speakers for the 8-track stereo are also heart-shaped, as is the base of the custom telephone by the bed and the loops of the chandelier hanging over it.

The pink carpeting throughout the van comes along the floor, up the walls, and around the ceiling in one continuous cocoon, the ultimate in wall to wall. But what finally slays you is the electric fireplace flickering in the corner. Now *that's* class. *Vantastic* is the automotive expression of the Me Decade.

"I like it this way," says Joe Doherty, proudly. "It expresses me." He is standing outside, his arm around his van. He is a mechanic by trade but sees himself as an artist. After work he spends his spare time working on *Vantastic*—a little more upholstery here, a mirror there. "I've always felt I had a talent for interior decoration," Joe says. It turns out he spends more time hanging around Bloomingdale's than garages.

Although *Vantastic* looks like a fancy whorehouse on wheels, Joe is adamant that he didn't build it with sex foremost in mind but because he loves vans. "A man doesn't put $20,000 into a truck to pick up a woman," Doherty is saying. "I think of this van as great architecture." Sure enough, on the coffee table in the living room is a copy of *Architectural Digest.*

Vantastic is a show van as opposed to a street van—about the same as the difference between a prize dog and a mutt. Street vans are custom also, as no serious vanner would consider driving anything that wasn't personalized. But street vans are less fancy and are used for work during the week and then cleaned up for the weekends. Show vans are never used for work. Doherty, in fact, rarely even drives his van—it was brought to this event on a trailer. "I can't take a chance with so many crazies on the road," Doherty says. "Not to mention the vandals."

Joe is most irate because "the world thinks vanners are a bunch of hippies and dope addicts. Hell," he says, "we're their number one victims." He shows me the sophisticated antiburglar equipment he has skillfully concealed all over *Vantastic.* "I've got to have it," he says. "No insurance company will insure the inside of a van."

Doherty is hoping to win first prize in the show van category. There are over a thousand vans here at the Englishtown, New Jersey gig, and the competition is fierce. Doherty is eyeing one with a second story built onto it. Nearby is another called *Chamber of Horrors,* which has eerie sounds coming from it, ghoulish paintings on its sides, and wooden tombstones and wired monsters set up inside. They say it has foolproof protection against someone trying to steal it. When you open the hood, mechanical bats fly out and there are bloodcurdling screams.

It's late June, and this event is called "Truckin' Into Summer." A truck-in or gig is about the same as a rally for other RVers. The main differences are that only vans are allowed here, almost everyone is young, almost everyone is drinking beer, and there are blacks and other minorities here—groups seldom seen at other RV rallies. This truck-in is taking place over a long weekend, and there are vans here from as far north as Vermont and as far south as Virginia. They're spread out in a huge field by the Englishtown racetrack, where some of the special events of the truck-in, such as van races and van tugs-of-war, take place. The field is covered with vans as far as the eye can see. In between the vans are campfires, people milling about amiably with beer cans in their hands, long lines waiting to get into the Portasans. Everyone's getting along with everyone else.

The stereo is on in most of the vans. The music of thirty AM and FM stations and infinite 8-track cassettes inundates the field in a cacophony of sound. Stands set up around the periphery of the field sell beer, bumper stickers, window-sized decals with tropical scenes, customized T-shirts. A young man in an apron and goggles is doing fine glass-etching work on vans which are lined up seeking his services. Right now he's using a tiny drill on the front vent windows of a black, otherwise undecorated van belonging to someone who just got into vanning. Next to the glass etcher a tattoo parlor is functioning. "This is a trucker's Woodstock," someone says.

"Maybe so," says Kathy Meyerhoffer, secretary of Ramapo Valley Truckers, "but we're responsible people." The Ramapo Valley Club has seventeen vans at this gig, set around in their own little circle, wagon-train style. All vans have their sliding doors open so that club members can visit back and forth. There is a community cooking fire in the middle of the circle, and a large parachute rigged for shade. Most of the members are married, and several have children with them. "We try to have a good reputation," says Leo DeVincenzi, president of the club. "If a trucker is married, he brings his old lady and children along to our events." The Ramapo club campsite seems as wholesome as a Fourth of July picnic.

Still, vanners are very sensitive about their public image. "Everybody thinks we're a bunch of Hell's Angels or something," DeVincenzi says, "but they're wrong. One of our members is a lawyer. Another is a teacher. We're anything but bums. Okay, so we like trucks and we like to drink beer, does that make us outlaws?" DeVincenzi told me that one of

Ramapo's main activities is raising money for Muscular Dystrophy. "What we've got," he said, "is good old-fashioned community spirit."

Most of Ramapo's members seem to be in the club for the social life it offers. "You go down to the corner bar," DeVincenzi says, "and it'll take an hour or so before you meet someone who thinks like you. But you come to a gig like this and, in addition to your own club, you've got three thousand people who think like you. You belong to something."

To show me what van clubs do, Kathy Meyerhoffer gives me Ramapo's schedule for July:

1 July–4 July	Unnatural Act III Gig. Western New York Van Association, Williamsville, New York
3 July	For those who stay home: Party at Don's house
5 July	Lower New York Van Council Meeting
6 July	Meeting. Dues due.
8 July	Some club members leaving for California
8 July–10 July	Weekend party, Rockland County Vanners
13 July	Meeting
15 July–17 July	Gig at Mohawk Race Track
20 July	Meeting
21 July–24 July	5th Annual National Truck-in. Campgrounds, Farmington, Massachusetts
23 July	Truck-in For Life. Beacon Hose #1 Ambulance Corp., Beacon, Connecticut

Just before Halloween, I went to a rally Ramapo Valley Truckers was sponsoring for vanners all over the East Coast, called "Truck O' Treat." A rally for vanners usually means a one-day motorized treasure hunt or obstacle course followed by a party. This one originated in the Korvette Shopping Plaza in

Nanuet, New York. I arrived late: most of the vans had already headed out. But Kathy Meyerhoffer found me a place in #285, the last van in line at the starting checkpoint.

This van was called *The Pinball Machine* because it had a disabled Japanese pachinko machine mounted in the back. Jeffrey Neiss, of Yonkers, New York, was driving, and Nancy Sawin, his girlfriend, was copilot. Jeffrey is a mechanic and Nancy is a student at Mercy College. "Van rallies give us a place to go," Nancy said.

Jeffrey said that before he discovered vanning he had "no direction." Now he plans to "stay in transportation one way or the other. I'm not going to sit behind a desk." Jeffrey's dream is to get money and time together for a cross-country trip in his van. He has been cross country twice, but that was with his parents and, he says with derision, "It was in a Chevy Impala." Like most vanners, Jeffrey calls his van "a truck" and has an affinity for trucks in general. "The bigger the better," he says. "Hell, I wouldn't mind having my own semi." What Jeffrey likes best about his van is the independence it gives him: "I can do whatever I want, wherever I go. You park this baby and you're *home.*"

It was an hour before *The Pinball Machine* was out of the parking plaza and onto the road. Each van had been given somewhat different instructions in a tricky code. To win the rally, a driver had to make forty-five correct decisions in a row and arrive at the finish line in the shortest elapsed time. Trophies were to be awarded to the winners.

We went roaring out, looking for clues. "At the sign of the bird make a right," was first on our instruction sheet. This was easy: a restaurant called The Rooster. "God Bless America and turn left." A home at an intersection with a flag in front of it. Wherever we went vans charged about the countryside, beeping at each other, some with musical horns which played the first few bars of "The Star Spangled Banner" or "Old McDonald's Farm." Occasionally a van passed us piloted by beavers, CB lingo for women.

After a few more clues, we found ourselves lost and had to retrace our steps. We made several more correct turns in a row only to find ourselves lost again. After three and a half hours, we had made it only up to number eleven on our instruction sheet. Jeff decided to give up the treasure hunt and head straight to the party.

Outside the roadhouse where the party was taking place, vans were scattered about the hillsides. Inside, two rock bands played simultaneously and hundreds of young vanners danced clumsily and drank the omnipresent beer. I could hardly push my way inside the building and decided, after ten minutes of earsplitting noise, to stay outside, where I met a heavyset guy named Ira Stoloff, a member of the Big Apple Van Club of Brooklyn.

Ira is a telephone repairman who drives a van all week for Bell Telephone. "But this one," Ira said, pounding on his van roof, "is my home away from home. If hell breaks loose in New York City, this is my getaway vehicle." I asked him what he meant by hell breaking loose. "Well," he said, "imagine a *three-day* power failure instead of the one day we had. Imagine that!"

Ira, whose CB handle is "The Tinman," and his wife Diane, whose handle is "The Golden Tongue," love their van club. "You know what this thing is?" Ira asks passionately. "It's a family, that's what. If I have trouble, one of the truckers in my club always helps me out. If he has trouble I help him. And I don't mean just with our trucks. I mean with money, personal problems, whatever. These are the nicest people in the world. Do you know what our biggest activity is as a club? Raising money for cancer!"

Ira's main beef, as is the case with most vanners, is that the general public sees vanners as disreputable, even criminal. "Do you know what we really are?" he asks. "Roving ambassadors of good will, that's what. Roving ambassadors of good will."

Then, as if to conclusively prove the van's respectability, Ira says, "The van is replacing the family station wagon, only people don't know it yet." He may be right. Wally Byam inadvertently pointed to this development when he predicted, in *Trailer Travel*

Here and Abroad, the creation of "larger, family-sized station wagons, self-contained and mass produced." Sales of station wagons have been plummeting in recent years and sales of vans have been skyrocketing. "VANS, WHERE THE NEXT ACTION IS," reads an auto industry circular.

At first, staid Detroit wanted nothing to do with vans—except as delivery vehicles—because it was afraid of identifying itself with oddballs. But as the demand for vans mounted, Detroit was forced to pay heed. During the 1974–1975 recession, the only type of vehicle which actually gained in sales was the van—so much so that Detroit changed it's advertising policy and began to promote vans as a "family vehicle." "Amen," said *Van Life and Family Trucking* magazine: "Who are van . . . people? They're your next door neighbors, that's who." Vans, like most things new to American society, started with youth and the minorities, got attention from the media, and then was adopted by the middle class.

Nevertheless, vans retain some of their connections with crime and sin in the popular mind. Television, that constant reflector of the prevailing wisdom, constantly puts bad guys in vans on such shows as "Starsky and Hutch" and "Baretta"—though, as vanners are quick to point out, the crooks usually have rented or stolen vans. The Hollywood movie, *The Van,* is the story of a young man of eighteen who buys a van for the sole purpose of picking up girls to seduce. He has a waterbed in the back of his van— reinforcing the van's occasional nicknames "Fucktruck" and "Fuckmobile"—even though a van could not carry that much weight over any distance, and the sloshing water in a waterbed would, after the van had gone around one or two turns, probably put the vehicle out of control.

A prominent news story several years ago did not help the van's reputation. It concerned prostitutes in New York using vans as rolling brothels. With chauffeurs up front, prostitutes would, by telephone arrangement, stop on Manhattan street corners to pick up well-heeled executives. The men, who commuted to work from Long Island or New Jersey, had sex

with the prostitutes in the back of the vans while being driven toward their homes, where they arrived at the usual time.

Vanners themselves don't always help the van's image. They combat their reputation as "bad boys," but they relish it as well. Many vans sport bumper stickers which say: "GAS, GRASS, OR ASS . . . NO ONE RIDES FREE." Others say "DON'T TOUCH THIS VEHICLE UNLESS YOU ARE COMPLETELY NUDE," or "DON'T LAUGH, YOUR DAUGHTER MAY BE IN THIS TRUCK." Still others sport decals with a picture of a nude woman which says "DO IT IN A VAN." John Burks, a writer sympathetic to vans, reinforces this image by constantly associating them with sex. In the book *Vans,* a young woman admits: "The girls knew that if they went out with a guy who had a van there would usually be something else involved. Because it's so convenient, it's right there. You don't have to hassle with a place to go. Most of the girls at my school lost their virginity in the back of a van. It was a joke in our school: you didn't lose your virtue correctly unless you did it in the back of a van."

The presumed raunchiness of the van world is underscored in an offensive advertisement which regularly appears in van magazines headed: "HAVE YOU EVER MADE LOVE TO AN UGLY WOMAN?" It continues:

> If the answer is yes, you probably did so because you knew your chances of getting what you wanted were far greater with an ugly broad than they could be with some foxy, phony good looking thing. So, next time you want to buy van parts, and you call the recreation vehicle warehouse, with the big, good looking ads and get the phony answers about why they won't give you what you want, remember your past triumphs and call the ugly little van parts warehouse in Cincinnati Ohio.

It's difficult to tell what women who are into vanning think about the attitudes this advertisement and the bumper stickers portray. Most vanners are blue-collar, and women who are into vanning are not the avant garde of contemporary feminism. Van clubs have Class A and Class B memberships. "A" members are van owners, and since most vans are owned by men, their wives and girl friends are invariably the "B" members—a cross between motorcycle mamas and the ladies auxiliary of the Rotarians. When Leo DeVincenzi, of Ramapo Valley Truckers, said to me, "The women in our club usually take care of all the bookkeeping and secretarial work," none of the "B" member women present objected. I have never heard a female vanner object to the term "beaver" (indeed, female vanners use the term almost as freely as men), and female vanners seem to see as much humor in the sexual nature of van bumper stickers and decals as do men. Occasionally, females do express a desire for there to be only one class of vanners, as in this verse from a poem published in a van newspaper, "Lament of 'Vanner's Wife' ":

> But it would please me greatly
> And be of good manners
> If my name could be added
> To the list of full-fledged vanners

Nevertheless, there are some women who own their own vans and are Class A members of van clubs. Jean DiTarranto, of Toms River, New Jersey, a professional hairdresser, drives a van and says that her only difficulty is forever having to explain that Covered Bridge, her van, is not a boyfriend's or husband's.

Whatever nascent feminism exists among vanners, it is usually expressed in a nonradical manner. This is partly because the adolescent sexuality projected by vanners is intermixed with their rebellion against Detroit's uniformity. Vans are the contemporary embodiment of the rogue vehicles of the past—the hot rods and custom cars of the 1950s and the motorcycles of the 1960s. An article in a van magazine, aping Tom Wolfe's famous essay on custom cars, "The Kandy-Kolored Tangerine-Flake Streamline Baby," describes the van as "the candy-colored, metal-flaked vinyl-button tucked, mean faced truck."

Middle-class America mistrusts individualized vehicles of any kind, but especially vans. So much so that police harassment of drivers of vans seems to be a given—regardless of civil liberties questions involved. While celebrating and granting status to individuality in homes, Americans seem threatened by individuality in vehicles—a strange contradiction in a society that prizes mobility above all else.

The origin of vans may explain this attitude in part. They were, like many newcomers to the American scene, a product of California—specifically of the surfer culture that emerged in the late 1960s as part of the dropout revolt against the Vietnam War and the work ethic. Identified with youth and the pleasure principle, vans were naturally suspect. When, in addition, vanners began decorating their vehicles in baroque styles, as if flaunting their counterculture status, they became a logical target for the forces of righteous conservatism.

While early vanners were sometimes consciously rebellious against the politics and mores of American society, more important to them was that they had found an inexpensive vehicle that was not only perfect for toting surfboards, but for living at the beach. It had a great deal more interior space than a station wagon and was infinitely more private, for it either had no windows in back or small, one-way windows that could be installed. More solidly built and powerful than a Volkswagen camper, it could be made as comfortable as a motor home. Finally, as a commercial vehicle, it fairly cried out for decoration and customizing. There was the challenge of taking something plain and everyday and creating a work of art.

Southern California became the center of van culture—so much so that by the early 1970s over 250 mini factories for converting vans were functioning in Los Angeles alone. Like all new ideas, which at first seem threatening, vanning not only became popular; it gradually became more respectable as well. Vanning culture moved to the East Coast and, from there, went out over network airwaves to the rest of the nation. "A new form of nomadness is sweeping the country," *Time* magazine announced. Detroit, sensing profits, began to come out with its own "custom" vans.

Today, van conversions are produced in four ways. Detroit has a few production models that differ from commercial vans only in their decorative pinstriping and plush interiors. Recreation vehicle manufacturers go further, raising roofs and installing some of the same equipment that goes into motor homes. Then there are special van conversion shops that work on only one or two vans at a time, producing completely individualized masterpieces at great cost. (Recently a Chevrolet van conversion was created for an Arab prince for $70,000 by Trix Magic Vans of East Orange, New Jersey.) Finally, there are van conversions that are created entirely by owners themselves.

Coachmen Industries, one of the major recreation vehicle manufacturers, has a van conversion plant in Middlebury, Indiana, which I visited. At the start of the assembly line, a sight made me cringe: a workman moved slowly around the van, decapitating it with a high-power saw, the way a brain surgeon removes the top of the skull. The roof was discarded, and at station two, a fiberglass roof was fastened in its place—raising the inside dimensions two feet and making it possible to stand upright in the van. At subsequent stations, the Detroit-installed seats were ripped out, insulation was foamed into all walls, wood paneling was attached to cover the insulation, velour bucket seats were bolted in and plush carpeting replaced the rubber matting, round holes were cut in the body toward the rear and bubble windows fitted, electrical and plumbing connections were made and LP refrigerators and stoves were installed. And so on. Toward the end of the line, the vans were covered with masking tape, supergraphics were sprayed on them, they were blower dried, and they were driven out into the sunshine.

Other RV companies add pop-up tops to vans, pop-out tentrooms in the rear of vans, and cabover compartments with double beds in them, producing a vehicle whose configuration is a cross between a van and a mini motor home; also added are tipout mini rooms that extend from the side of the van to form a double bed compartment when parked.

Still, "true vanners" won't touch what they call a "pro" van—

one which comes off any kind of assembly line, Detroit or Elkhart—regarding those who drive them as impossibly conservative and conformist. "They've taken all the fun out of trucking," one young vanner said to me. With more acceptance of vans as family travel vehicles, van purists are driven to further extremes in their designs—but then, Detroit and Elkhart simply go into production with good imitations. Not too far into the 1980s, I suspect, a new kind of rogue vehicle will replace the van as the cult object of the young.

Meanwhile, people are finding more and more uses for vans. Veterinarian Charles Kaufman, who lives in Brooklyn, uses his as a mobile pet hospital. Making only house calls, Kaufman is prepared to do emergency surgery in his van—especially for cats or dogs that have been hit by a car. Vans are increasingly being used by large corporations as car pool vehicles. In Nebraska, a van converter is producing red and white N vans with complete bars aboard for University of Nebraska football rooters who like to go to the games in style. The van's horn plays the first line of "There Is No Place Like Nebraska." Vans with bubble tops are being converted for use as ice cream and other kinds of vending trucks. Vans with wheelchair lifts are finding ready application for the handicapped (as in the television series "Ironside").

As cars are downsized, vans are also becoming *the* vehicle for towing trailers. Since they are classified "commercial," vans meet lower federal MPG standards. Several RV manufacturing companies are marketing van-trailer packages, where the van interior and exterior have been decorated to match the trailer's.

Vans have proven to be ideal vehicles for those embarking on long-distance trips. Harry Coleman and Peggy Larson of Los Angeles took a twenty month round-the-world trip in a van. They covered 143,716 miles and 113 countries. They were robbed in Rio de Janeiro, charged by an elephant in Kenya, threatened with imprisonment and whipping for bringing liquor into Saudi Arabia, and stuck in the sand seventeen times while crossing the Sahara. But, they say, "We learned and saw more than most people do in a lifetime."

Others use their vans to live in a more stationary way. Butch Campbell, of Ocean Grove, New Jersey, gave up his $300-a-month apartment and fixed up a van for himself that he keeps parked in his parents' driveway. Butch eats most of his meals out and showers in his parents' house. He works nearby as a cabinetmaker and does very little driving other than going back and forth to work. "Sure the van is my vehicle," Butch says, "but it's even more my home."

Butch's life-style suggests an aspect of van culture which differs from that of other RVs. The vanner is often content not to go anywhere at all—just to stay in his van. It's often said that Americans are so mobility-oriented that the trip itself is more important to them than the destination. They just like *to go.* In the van we see this carried further. For the vanner, not even the trip is necessary—for the destination is the van itself, that gorgeous womb with a view out on the far edge of American fantasy land, a personal pleasure den. As one vanner said to me, "Whoever said it was un-American to build yourself a beautiful home? If mine's on wheels, that's because I like it that way. Pleasure is coming back."

The back door of a homebuilt.

Chapter VII
Do-It-Yourself

We knew nothing and had to figure it out.
That seems to be the true way.

Stephen Gaskin, spiritual leader of The Farm
Commune, Summertown, Tennessee, speaking to the
author about the converted buses in which most
commune members first lived

While vanners, of all RVers mentioned thus far, are the most innovative, there is a group that goes further—the folks who build their own homes on wheels from scratch. One of them—Mick O'Bird, an elderly gentleman with a welding business in Ceres, California—wrote to me at length. In the account that follows, I have left his spelling and punctuation intact.

I have been building . . . house cars since 1925 and have tried living on wheels since 1903. First trip with a team of horses and a wagon with a tent on it from Ann arbor Michigan . . . to Bradley Michigan. Took 16 days to go 128 miles. In 1925 bought a Cincenatti, Dayton and Hamilton Ohio Inter City Bus. Used. 4 cylinder Reo. Took out the seats and made a house car out of it. It was not an original idea with me. Some years before I talked with three men that I met . . . fishing on the Ausable River out of Grayling Michigan. They had a house car built on a one ton Ford truck with cabinets, beds, grub boxes and a wood stove. I told them that someday I would have one of those. They asked me my name and I told them that I was Mick O'Bird. One man told me to be sure to get a Ford truck. I asked him why. He said "I am Henry Ford and this is Harvy Firestone and this is thomas Edison." * That house car sold me on that kind of camping right there. So when I saw that bus for sale in Cincenatti I just had to buy it and make my house car. . . . I used a three burner oil stove to cook on; smelly dam thing. Put it right behind the drivers seat on the left side. Table accross from the stove. Bed accross the back under the rear window. . . . It sure ran nice. I got a job with the Lincoln Electric Co. in Buffalo N.Y. . . . and lived in the bus-housecar. But it got too cold to stay in the bus so in December 1925 We left Buffalo and headed south for Columbus Ohio in a rain storm. . . . By the time we got to the hill going down into Akron the road was just a glare of ice. We skidded 2–3 miles banging off this curb and that like slow motion and very helpless. . . . The

* Ford, Firestone, and Edison were friends and often went on camping trips together.

only causulty was our supper warming on the stove. A can of Van Camps pork and beans, a can of Dinty'Mores Stew and a pot of coffee. All of that landed on the floor. Our great Dane Dog was so disgusted he wouldn't even help us clean it up. I saw then that the stove should be on the right side because it's the low side of the highway, and have a pot rail around it. . . . The next summer we headed west. Got as far as Midland Texas when I got a job welding in a new town 31 miles straight south of there. They said all I had to do was follow the tracks where the trucks were hauling pipe and material to build a refinery and town. I put a gallon of cleaning solvent into my tank and started out. I couldn't do anything *but* follow the tracks. A lot of those miles my axles and differential draged in the sand. I ran out of gas and had to be towed the last three miles into town. But I was the envy of everyone else. I had brought my house-car with me, but they were living in tents. The pipe and fittings were being supplied by "The Crane Pipe and Fitting Co." So they called the town Crane. It's still called Crane. We stayed there till the next summer, but it got too hot so we decided to head back east. The road had been improved so we got back out that 31 miles okay. Got clear to Dallas before we stopped at a little tourist camp by a creek as we were coming into town. . . . Saw in the Dallas paper that the Ford Assembly plant wanted a cutter and welder. They were making Model As now, not Ts. So I went out there and told them what I could do. . . . That evening a bus came into the camp. It was really nice, built on a White truck chassis larger than mine. It had a chaufuer colored and colored maid and was all built up for living. So I wandered over to look it over and then turned to my wife and said "I think I know that man." So I asked him, "Isn't your name Kellog?" He said "Yes. And you look familiar too."* So

* O'Bird is referring to W. K. Kellogg, the breakfast-food king, whose custom motor home was built on a 1923 White Motor truck chassis and fitted with a shower, a lavatory, a stove, and central heating. Kellogg called his motor home The Ark and used to say, "When I'm tired of making cornflakes, I find The Ark an incentive to rest."

I told him "I used to sit on your lap when my step father and I used to come over to Kalamazoo to trade horses." He said, "Good gosh Your all grown up. Look Ma! Here is! Here's Mick! . . . " We sat and talked half the night. Didn't have time for breakfast and had to cook in the house car on the way to work the next morning. During the night Mr. Kellog told me that they were just coming back from California. . . . Stayed on that job about three weeks untill one day the work seemed to run out so I decided to go to Detroit. . . . Crossed the Mississippi river and turned north, intending to do some fishing in Reelfoot Lake. But night came on so, we bedded down. . . . In about an hour the big Dane dog nudged me with his nose and I felt the car move. I quieted him and got the flashlite and the rifle. I opened the door very quietly. Said "Get Em" and stepped out on the groind. There were three of them and they had one tire off and were taking off the other one on the rear. The big Dane knocked two of them down and held them. The other took one look at the 175 pound Great Dane and fainted. I let the first two up and made them put the tires back on by themselves. Now I'm only 5 feet 4 inches tall but . . . I told them I didn't like them and that they should have taken up some other trade. Then I slapped each of them flat handed and knocked them down and drove off and left those three nice young men lying there on the blacktop. Got into Indianapolis the next day. Never did fish in Reelfoot Lake. Went on into Detroit and got a job with the Titus Welding Co. . . . We stayed there till Nov. 15th 1928. Then came out to California. Got here Dec 3rd 1928, been here ever since. Since then I have owned and used trailers of most every kind except mobile homes. Nothing that I have to hire someone else to moove for me. One of the nicest ones that I built was for a young inventor by the name of Larsen. . . . He had a plymouth Roadster and we made it to be pulled by that. We made the trailer frame and body out of 3/4 inch light conduct pipe with a goosneck front end on it. Covered it with chicen wire netting, then cotton padding and finally Panasote auto top fabric. We used the ball off a Mack truck torque arm and welded the ball socket to a plate that bolted to the center of the spare wheel that laid flat in the turtle back behind the seat. He got a patent on it and took it east and sold the manufacturing rights to Glen curtice.* Curtice wanted them to transport pasingers from the hotels out to the air fields. . . . I've often thought of making another trailer like that again but Plymouth Roadsters are hard to find lately. . . . One time I built a very small house car, made of a U.S. walkin mail van truck, with a two burner Sterno Canned Heat stove. That was 11 years ago. I saw it again the other day and the man's son and his new wife were using it to travel on their honeymoon. I tried to buy it back. They just laughed at me. They had given it a new paint job and new carpets and curtains, but it still had the Sterno Stove, handoperated water pump, single cavity sink and candle sticks that I installed when I built it when the boy was eleven years old. I asked them "Why?" They told me that it represented the difference between being able and not being able to go to college. And the whole thing began as a joke to see how reasonable I could build it and how cheap it would operate. It still gets a little over 17 miles to the gallon of gasoline. . . . It has 152,756 actual miles on it, and that's pretty good for a 1952 Dodge Walkin van. I'm copying down the prices of the van and the main components used to put the house car together in 1966. I think some of these prices will be a little higher now. But it will show what can be done with a little determination and perseveriance. After all, "Poverty is the mother of invention, and Necessity is his father."

Sharps Government Surplus Lathrop Calif.,
1 used mail Dodge Van		$209.00
San Jose Flea Market, Porta potty		70.00
Used sink $15.00 + stove $35.00		50.00
2 used windows	$10.00 each	20.00

* Glen Curtiss, the World War I airplane designer, built a number of trailers in the late 1920s called Aerocars and used for transporting passengers to and from airplanes.

3 sheets 3/8 x 4x8 plywood	$8.00 each	24.00
2 sheets 1/4 x 4x8 plywood	$6.00 each	12.00
4 metal closet door slides		12.00
toilet door hinges and door latch, screen door type		6.00
1 used spare wheel and tire		10.00
motor tune up, plugs, points and wires		12.00
hand water pump, (used)		3.00
1 gallon Rustoleum paint outside		9.00
1 gallon white trim inside		10.00
Rug remnants to completely cover inside		20.00
		$467.00

Or maybe it's the other way around; "Necessity is the Mother of invention and Poverty is the Father." And in my case I've had my share of both. After all I started out living in homebuilts when they was all that was available. Maybe that's why I sometimes think that some of the class A motor homes go a little overboard when they call their products campers. Camping is not like that at all. Even some modern homes are not as delux or plush or expensive. I once built a fancy motorhome for myself out of a bus I got from Government Surplus. I Built it to finish raising the rest of my five children, so I did a good job on the insides. The kids are all gone now so I sold it to a friend of mine who has a machine shop for $10,000.00 and he is useing it to intertane customers and help raise his grand children while my youngest son, just out of the U.S. Marines, runs his machine shop for him. The past two weeks he has been in southern Arizona with his wife and one grand child. He called me to laugh at me here in the cold central California valley and tell me that he had just installed a Wood Stove and how much fun he was haveing while we were freezing here in the cold fog. Well I guess I'll haveto close and mail this while it is still portable. If you use any of this you may have to treat it like a tree. Prune it and trim it till it fits. . . .

Yours very truly
Mick O'Bird

I hope Mick likes the way I have pruned and trimmed his letter. It sure has style—and maybe even a bit of the American tall tale too. I've included as much of Mick's odyssey as possible because it expresses so well the passion and innovativeness of those who build homes on wheels themselves—the do-it-yourselfers.

In a sense, everyone into RVs is a do-it-yourselfer and most RV companies were founded by someone who built himself an RV, then built one for a friend or neighbor, and then went into manufacturing. And this is still happening. All over the country, but especially in towns in Indiana, Michigan, and California, backyards and garages hum with the work of amateur inventors who will be tomorrow's tycoons of the RV industry.

Doug Richardson, of Malibu, California, converted a British Land Rover for use as a mini motor home. He was intent on making it as comfortable as possible without sacrificing off-road performance. It worked so well that he now is converting his thirteenth and has begun to have a tidy little business.

George and Meda Durepo, of Lee, New Hampshire, built a trailer for themselves some years ago and then, when they craved more space, built a larger one. After building the two units they had so many parts left over, they had "no choice but to go into the parts and accessories business which is doing quite well." They're now planning to build a fifth wheel of thirty-five or forty feet, large enough to take their business—called "Not A Kit," same name as their trailers—on the road.

There are some who *do* build their own RVs from kits. The Glen-L Company, of Bellflower, California, sells ready-to-assemble kits—for trailers, fifth wheels, truckcampers, pickup covers, and van conversions—which they ship to you. The Scamp Company, of Backus, Minnesota, sells component parts for a small, fiberglass trailer that can be towed by a Volkswagen. You can also get plans for an RV in *Popular Mechanics,* which regularly publishes them for all kinds of small RVs as does the Trail-R Club of America in Beverly Hills, California.

Despite the availability of plans and kits, most RVers

determined to build their own go all the way—with plans and components of their own design. W.H. Martin, of Hammond, Indiana, built his own motor home from scratch on a Dodge M300 chassis when he retired at age sixty-two in 1970. He says he also built the "laundry" in his motor home, a large diaper pail filled with soap and water which "makes a good agitator washing machine while you're driving." Roy White, of San Bernardino, California, built himself a motor home but, like most of us, made some mistakes. He hooked up the flush toilet to the hot water tank. "My wife decided to give the new toilet an initiation. When she flushed the toilet she let out a yell. Hot water and steam emitted from the john."

White, who is sixty-eight and has a forty-year-old wife and a new baby, slowly came around to wanting to build his own motor home. "For a number of years, I've spent my vacations camping and fishing. First with tents. Then I decided to build a trailer to set the tent on. In the summer of 1975, I rented a Scotty seventeen-foot trailer for a trip to Minneapolis, Minnesota. On the return trip I told the wife I was going to build a motor home when we got back to California." Like other do-it-yourselfers, White takes a great deal of pride in his work: "I'm so satisfied with the results, I'd challenge any commercial makers to get as much floor space, window, and cubic feet of cupboard space in a unit this size."

Marshall Sanders of Hamilton, Montana, must be one of the more ingenious of the do-it-yourselfers. He built a motor home called *Ultra Motion* by combining the body of a thirty-three-foot 1946 Spartan trailer with the chassis from a wrecked Oldsmobile Toronado with front wheel drive. Gutting the trailer and cutting its front wall out, he found that the powerful Oldsmobile engine matched the shell of the trailer perfectly, so that all he had to do was bolt them together. With that combination, Sanders was able "to steer this monster with one-finger effort."

Building almost from scratch, Sanders was able to decorate to suit his fancy. The door of the motor home is made from old barn wood. The desk is made out of a wine barrel and has a nail keg for a seat. There is a bright orange, cone-shaped fireplace. Sanders excited so much interest in Ultra Motion that he now finds himself building RVs for others. So far he has converted a 1948 twenty-nine-passenger Flexible bus and a 1962 International school bus into motorcoaches.

Converting buses has long been a favorite device of those interested in a distinctive home on wheels. Buses are large, powerful, and ruggedly built. With seats, overhead racks, and passengers removed, the total weight to be added—including appliances, beds, a false floor to fill in the aisle, etc.—does not begin to approximate the vehicle's limits. Buses are a step up from the manufactured motor home. As the title of a recent article in *Popular Mechanics* put it, "Outgrown Your Motorhome? Take The Bus."

In the 1960s, converted buses became identified with the hippie movement as communes-on-wheels. The Farm, a commune of a thousand young people near Nashville, Tennessee, was founded by a bus caravan of people from the Haight Ashbury in San Francisco, many formerly part of the hard-drug scene, who followed their guru, Stephen Gaskin, around the country until they located in Summertown, Tennessee.

In his book, *The Caravan,* Stephen describes life on the road before the founding of The Farm: "We were . . . in a caravan of . . . better than fifty great buses, and we were this giant organism on the freeway right in the vein of society. They'd built these huge rest stops that swallow up semi's, and we just filled them from one end to the other. . . . We'd make a town, stay a couple of hours, do all our groceries, and meet at the next rest stop on the other side of town and truck on. We went twelve thousand miles like that."

In Minneapolis, Stephen's address to the congregation of a Catholic Church included these remarks: "Well, some Minneapolis police came into the parking lot yesterday. . . . They just came out to talk to us, and one of them said he felt like taking off his coat and badge and getting a school bus

Outside the house.

and joining the caravan, and as they left, the other one said, 'Maybe we'll go refinance our houses and get schoolbuses.' One of them kept saying, 'It's like Huck Finn, you know?' "

What Stephen called his "traveling monastery," trucked for four months, and "finally we got back to San Francisco and something had happened to us. We had metamorphosed. We weren't quite city folks anymore. We pulled into San Francisco and said, 'There's no place to park, man, where we gonna put the caravan?' We had two Sunday Morning Services and one Monday Night Class in San Francisco. On the second morning I announced that it was a driver's meeting, and we were going to stow and go, we were going to go find a farm, because we'd become a village on the road."

On The Farm today many of the buses have given way to houses, but in the early years of the commune members lived in their buses, most of which, once parked, never moved again. A few years ago I spent a week as the guest of some friends who had settled on The Farm and were still living in a bus. They liked to tell the story of how their converted school bus had made it to the front gates of The Farm and "dropped dead"; it had to be pushed to their homesite. It was cozy in the bus that week. There was a spaceheater which vented through the roof. Running water flowed in by gravity from the mini-water tower my friend, Robert Scarola, had built outside. Robert and Nancy's son Russell played happily in his playpen in the middle of the bus.

California has always spawned the wildest of bus transformations, including buses totally shingled on the outside, buses with stained glass windows, buses with antique door handles and knockers, buses with lofts and back porches. Ken Kesey, the author of *One Flew Over The Cuckoo's Nest* and *Sometimes A Great Notion,* once traveled about the country with a California hippie group called the Merry Pranksters in a psychedelically painted bus. Tom Wolfe has described their experiences in his documentary novel *The Electric Kool-Aid Acid Test:* "I couldn't tell you for sure which of the Merry Pranksters

A professor of physics and his wife at home in their bus.

got the idea for the bus. . . . Somebody . . . saw a classified ad for a 1939 International Harvester school bus. The bus belonged to a man in Menlo Park . . . [with] eleven children. He had rigged out the bus for the children. It had bunks and benches and a refrigerator and a sink for washing dishes and cabinets and shelves and a lot of other nice features for living on the road. Kesey bought it for $1500—in the name of Intrepid Trips, Inc."

Kesey's plans for the bus-home were unusual. It would be an ambulatory media commune:

> Kesey gave the word and the Pranksters set upon it one afternoon. They started painting it and wiring it for sound and cutting a hole in the roof and fixing up the top of the bus so you could sit up there in the open air and play music, even a set of drums and electric guitars and electric bass and so forth, or just ride. Sandy went to work on the wiring and rigged up a system with which they could broadcast from inside the bus, with tapes or over microphones, and it would blast outside over powerful speakers on top of the bus. There were also microphones outside that would pick up sounds along the road and broadcast them inside the bus. There was also a sound system inside the bus so you could broadcast to one another over the roar of the engine and the road. You could also broadcast over a tape mechanism so that you said something, then heard your own voice a second later in variable lag and could rap off of that if you wanted to. Or you could put on earphones and rap simultaneously off sounds from outside, coming in one ear, and sounds from inside, your own sounds, coming in the other ear. There was going to be no goddam sound on that whole trip outside the bus, inside the bus, or inside your own freaking larynx, that you couldn't tune in on and rap off of.
>
> The painting job, meanwhile, with everybody pitching in in a frenzy of primary colors, yellows, oranges, blues, reds, was . . . freaking lurid. The manifest, the destination sign in the front, read: "Furthur," with two *u*'s. . . .

So the Hieronymous Bosch bus headed out of Kesey's place with the destination sign in front reading "Furthur" and a sign in the back saying "Caution: Weird Load." . . . The joints were going around, and it was nice and high out here on the road in America. . . .

Haul ass . . . out across the Southwest, and all of it on film and on tape. Refrigerator, stove, a sink, bunk racks, acid, speed, grass—with Hagen handling the movie camera and everybody on microphones and the music blaring out over the roar of the bus, rock 'n' roll.

Riding the bus was equivalent to being a member of a community. Kesey said: " 'Now, you're either on the bus or off the bus. If you're on the bus, and you get left behind, then you'll find it again. If you're off the bus in the first place—then it won't make a damn.' And nobody had to have it spelled out for them. Everything was becoming allegorical, understood by the group mind, and especially this: 'You're either on the bus . . . or off the bus.' "

The driver of the bus was Neal Cassady, model for the character of Dean Moriarity in Jack Kerouac's 1957 novel *On the Road*. But now it was the 1960s, and the solitary travel the beat generation popularized—the lone individual out there on the road with his thumb raised—was no longer in. What was in was all the group and communitarian activities of the 1960s—anti-war, anti-racism, the beginnings of the women's movement, the Woodstock nation. The kind of travel that went with it was community travel. First, hippies bought up VW campers and traveled about and lived in them. Then they moved on to buses. When Kesey spoke about being "on the bus or off the bus," much more was intended than whether someone was physically on the bus. Being on the bus meant associating oneself with an entire set of values and assumptions that grew out of an LSD-fueled grouphead. Being on the bus was a political act.

Not that converting buses is the province of hippies alone. John and Winnona Woodbury, of South Portland, Maine, have converted an old school bus into a traveling home. John is a truck driver, so you'd think the last thing he'd want to do on vacation is live in a bus. But, no, whenever he isn't working, he, Winnona, and their four children pile into their bus and hit the road. They have a 1966 International which they bought for all of $450 and have since put upwards of $6000 into. The Woodburys have plans, says Winnona: "When our youngest grows up we're going to live in the bus full time and take off for the hills. What we've got here is a ranch house on wheels— minus the taxes."

From hippie buses on one extreme, through the carefully crafted buses converted by individuals, one finally gets to motor coaches turned into luxury homes by professionals. These can cost as much as $200,000. Often they are made for upwardly mobile (pun half-intended) executives or doctors who have progressed from a tent trailer, through a mini motor home, through a large motor home such as a Landau or Executive, and are finally ready to graduate to the best the industry has to offer: a forty-foot long land yacht made to order for them, equipped with a rear-mounted (therefore quieter) diesel motor, and built more solidly than even the most luxurious motor homes.

Bus conversions are also created for VIP entertainment (stewardesses and all) by corporations such as McDonald's, which has a dozen of them; or they are made for traveling evangelists who, like nineteenth-century horseback preachers, ride about the country in "gospel coaches"; or for show business personalities. Elvis Presley had a converted bus which served as his dressing room and, sometimes, living quarters wherever he performed or was making a movie. For Presley, this was a must, since he was terrified of flying.

Converted buses are owned by a good number of country music performers, including Conway Twitty, Jeannie C. Riley, Roy Clark, and Merle Haggard. Milo Liggett left his career as a country music sideman years ago to spend full time building bus conversions in Nashville after he had successfully built one for his boss, Sonny James. "Back then," says Milo, "we didn't do much but put bunks in for the guys and make sure there was a table to play cards. The boys are making a little more money these days and have bigger ideas."

For performers the bus provides a home environment on exhausting road trips; and the entire cost is depreciable. The movie, *Coal Miner's Daughter,* portrays country music singer Loretta Lynn's life on and off her converted bus. Some country music singers rack up a quarter million miles a year traveling in their buses—so, however luxuriously outfitted, they are worth every penny. Waylon Jennings has a particularly luxurious bus. To give you an idea: the bathroom has twenty-four-karat gold-plated fixtures, a sculptured marble commode, a crushed velvet headliner, and a gold-plated star on the door. But the bit of luxury which means the most to Jennings is the painting of a rural scene that hangs just above the driver and meets Jennings's eye each time he gets on and off the bus—as if to remind him of what he is singing about.

A number of actors use converted buses while on location as personalized dressing rooms and living quarters. The late John Wayne had a bus with a great deal of tooled leather upholstery as befit his cowboy roles. TV actor Darold Westbrook has a 1950-vintage converted Greyhound that he uses for more than work. A member of the Southern California chapter of Bus Nuts, Westbrook attends all the bus and motor home rallies he can. "You lose a lot of friends this way," says Westbrook. "All my old friends wanted to talk about was show biz. But you gain a lot of new friends too. All they want to talk about is how to get ten MPG out of a 225 Cummins Diesel with 59,500 miles on it."

Some show business personalities rent bus-homes instead of buying them. As I write this, Kris Kristofferson and his wife, Rita Coolidge, are on tour in a bus they rented from Qonexions, a Secaucus, New Jersey firm which buys new MCI buses and outfits them so as to be able to transport, bed, and even feed large rock bands while on the road. Qonexions buses have been rented to transport such performers and their entourages as The Beach Boys, Boston, Neil Diamond, Barry Manilow, and Natalie Cole. Some Qonexions buses log over a hundred thousand miles a year and, to date, they have never broken down, since they have backup systems such as two complete sets of wiring and a large Onan generator that can handle *any* electric needs. If a bus ever does get into trouble, it has a radio telephone to summon aid. Calling themselves "The Secaucus Qonexion," Qonexions advertises in show business publications, offering "the perfect answer for how to gig in 35 cities in 40 days with all the comforts of home." An outfit similar to Qonexions, Loch Raven Coach, operating out of Nashville, Tennessee, specializes in country musician rentals and advertises under the motto "Home Is Where Your Bus Is!"

Some bus converters buy wrecks to rebuild or buy used buses direct from Greyhound or Trailways. Both of these companies have offices which do nothing but handle sales of their used buses, advertising regularly in RV industry publications. Elvin and Jeanette Bale, performers with Ringling Brothers and Barnum & Bailey Circus, bought a used bus from Continental Trailways in Dallas for $25,000 and then had Angola Coach, in Angola, Indiana, convert the bus into a traveling home for an additional $45,000. Elvin Bale is a trapeze artist and Jeanette Bale puts Lippizaner stallions through their paces. They are on the road ten and a half months of the year, so the bus is their regular home.

The Bales' bus has two bedrooms, an entry hall, a living room, a complete kitchen and full bath—all luxuriously outfitted. Floors are carpeted throughout, the ceiling is in padded white vinyl, there's a color TV, a microwave oven, a built-in dishwasher, and a well-stocked pantry. Elvin says, "What's unique about our motor coach is when friends stop by they . . . walk into the living room just as you would in a home. We've entertained as many as 10 guests in the living room at one time and all were surprised how comfortable it was." Although Elvin and Jeanette, given their professions, do very little drinking, their favorite accessory is a hydraulic pop-up bar in the living room. At the flip of a switch, five bottles of liquor and glasses appear.

Interested in how a bus could be converted into a luxury

personal home, I visited Angola Coach to see for myself. It is located in a shed-like building on State Road 127 two miles north of Angola—one of the many RV towns in northern Indiana. On the wall in the office is the familiar motto: "The Only Difference Between Men and Boys Is The Price Of Their Toys." In the factory, a bus, with wiring, plumbing, and carpentry proceeding simultaneously, was being converted into a showroom–home for a businessman who travels the country selling westernwear.

Beatrice and Phil Robertson, who own Angola Coach, have their own converted bus in which they take two vacations a year—to Florida for a month in the winter and out West in the summer. Don Macey, Willard Kime, and Gale Robertson, Phil's son, the three other people who work at Angola Coach, all have their own bus-homes too. Willard was a high school teacher for some years, but gave it up because kids "aren't like they used to be. They won't listen to nobody." Beatrice Robertson was also a teacher when she met Phil. She discovered she liked working with her hands and that making bus-homes "was just as challenging and creative as music."

Phil Robertson converted a bus for himself in 1965, taking on a rusting 1938 Flexible that was being used as a chicken coop by a farmer. Someone saw Phil's coach and asked him to build them one. Soon he had built three or four. He liked the work so much that, when more orders came in, he gave up his auto bodyshop and went into bus conversions full-time. His efforts were aided by the national concern over energy: as America became more mass transit-oriented, converting buses became more fashionable. The 1973–1974 and 1979 oil crises created a still greater demand for diesel-powered buses, and Angola had as much business as it could handle. Corporations purchasing bus conversions to transport executives and clients in style to meetings or football games now had their own "mass transit" facilities—and a tax write-off to boot!

Angola Coach takes about three months to convert a bus to a customer's specifications. Clients approach them—sometimes with a bus ready to convert, other times seeking a bus. Angola gets buses for clients from small charter companies whose buses haven't received the wear, and have been better maintained, than Greyhound's. The client usually has some kind of floor plan in mind and a notion of the kinds of rooms, furniture, and appliances he'd like to have. Appliances may include a central vacuum system, air conditioners, an intercom system throughout the bus, an icemaker, a washer and drier, a microwave oven, a stereo system, a trash compacter, and a waste destruction system that allows for sanitary disposal of toilet and other wastes while underway. The waste is slowly liquefied by the action inside the holding tank and then pumped into the vehicle exhaust system, where it mixes with the extremely hot exhaust gases and is destroyed at the rate of one gallon per fifteen miles of driving. One individual even had Angola install a Baldwin organ. Angola works with the client, making suggestions, until a final plan is agreed upon. Over the next months, the client is expected to show up every few weeks to make sure the work is proceeding according to mutual agreement. An Angola conversion, with exterior as well as interior modifications, costs between thirty-five thousand and eighty thousand dollars (plus the cost of the bus).

Though bus conversions have only recently been getting attention as the ultimate in RVs, they've been around for a long time by industry standards. In fact, buses were being converted well before the industry began producing motor homes, and Class A motor homes are really manufactured imitations of converted buses. The Family Motor Coach Association was founded by twenty-six school bus converters in 1963, when motor homes were still in their infancy.

Today, most members of FMCA are motor homers, but the "illustrious" members, the ones everyone knows, are bus converters. Mickey and Irene Braun probably have the most unusual vehicle in the association, a double-decker bus called *The Answer*. The Brauns wanted to combine full-time life on the road with enough space to live luxuriously. They purchased a school bus and built a second floor on it which can be raised and lowered hydraulically, giving them a total of 475 square feet of interior space. Mickey, a retired Navy aviator, handled the engineering; Irene handled the decoration. The two floors are connected by an interior staircase, and the top floor has a 9 x 8 patio-porch of cedar and redwood built on the back where the Brauns can sun themselves. The interior features raftered ceilings, bleached cypress paneling, a built-in bar, and a bathroom of Carrara marble.

The process of lowering or raising the upper level takes only fifteen minutes. The only rearranging necessary for lowering the roof is the removal of the curtain rods and curtains from the walls and the placing of such objects as the television set on the floor. When the ceiling is down, there are almost three feet of crawl space in the upper level, so the Brauns can still get something from upstairs. Whenever the Brauns pull in somewhere they raise the second floor into position, put up the curtains, and hang an American flag on their rear patio. On the road, *The Answer* is thirteen feet high, just within lawful limits. Parked, it is over seventeen feet high. When the Brauns first pulled into an FMCA rally with *The Answer*, RVers practically fell out of their buses and motor homes gawking at the sight.

Today the FMCA has a national office in Cincinnati, publishes *Family Motor Coaching* magazine, and has thirty-one thousand members in 130 chapters. To qualify for membership, a vehicle must be self-propelled and at least eighteen feet long, self-contained—meaning that it has an onboard sanitary system and everything it may need to function without external plumbing and electrical sources—and it must be built so that an adult can walk upright from the driver's seat to the back. Trailers, pickup campers, vans and the smaller motor homes are excluded.

Once a year, FMCA has a national rally to which thousands of bus converters and motor homers go—no matter where it is in the United States. The Robertsons, of Angola Coach, always build their summer vacation around the FMCA convention. *Time* magazine visited the 1978 rally, which was held in Sioux Falls, South Dakota. *Time* talked about the passion of the RVers at the rally, concluding: "They may be the largest extended family in America."

Chapter VIII
Full-Timers

I'll never own another house as long as I live

*Alfred Sevilla, formerly of Paducah, Kentucky,
now living in a trailer somewhere on the road in
America*

I got a letter the other day from a guy by the name of Ernie Beem of Bella Vista, California. Actually, Ernie doesn't live in Bella Vista; he has a post office box there. Ernie lives in a converted bus. It's a thirty-five-foot interstate transit bus which he has converted into a home.

Ernie used to live in a 1959 Ford Metro Delivery Van. He tore the racks out of the former bread truck and installed a 110-volt AC and 12-volt DC electrical system, a recirculating chemical toilet, a three burner stove with a 6 cubic-foot refrigerator underneath, an LPG space heater, and a bed. But the van "was a bit small for a permanent residence," so Ernie bought the bus.

Living in a van and a bus are new to Ernie. As he explained in his letter, it happened this way:

> In March of 1978 through a situation I had no control over I found myself and my dog Killer out on the street with no where to go. I had been living with a woman for six and a half years. We were buying a sixty thousand dollar home, we both had good jobs, you know, the typical west coast family. Seemingly over night it sort of fell apart and due to the wisdom of the california courts I got a 1972 Ford station wagon and my dog and she got everything else!
>
> Having only the Station Wagon and my dog I was unable to come up with a deposit on an apartment and couldn't find one that would take Killer anyway. I went to the local auto dismantler and traded the 1972 Ford Gran Torino Station wagon for a 1959 Ford Metro Van. . . .
>
> What this all boils down to is that after my home broke up I decided *I'll never live in something I can't take with me,* and in the process I found something I really enjoy doing.

Ernie Beem is a full-timer, an RVer who has no other home but his rig—and likes it that way. But lest the impression be given that such a life-style is suitable only for the young, here are excerpts from a letter to me by Mrs. E. R. Holter, whose return address is a P.O. Box in Carrollton, Texas:

We are now full time, retired, RV'ers. . . . We are not very interesting people but we have learned much.

We started RVing on vacation with 5 kids and a 17' Mobile Scout in 1963. As the children grew we added a tent for sleeping. We have six children—all grown now—but when we get together and share memories, they all remember camping as the greatest time of their lives. We are a close family, and . . . I think our cohesiveness goes back to the times we camped—where all shared the load of the work but each was free to do what he liked in spare time. . . .

I worked outside the home as soon as all were in school and long before women's lib became the mania it is today. I advanced to becoming the manager of a male dominated clinic of five doctors of medicine plus full lab, X ray and emergency room facilities. . . . Then suddenly my husband was disabled by a heart attack. By this time we had traded & worked our way up to a 32' fifth wheel trailer. My husband insisted on selling *every*thing and just traveling in our trailer.

I was devastated. I of course, was forced to retire to be with him. I was frantic!! I knew I would be bored, I was afraid of so much leisure and I *could not* give up the house that was the base of our family.

My husband is a good natured man (as long as he gets his own way) but no matter how I stormed-cried-pleaded-even pointed out that I would ruin his retirement if I was forced to be idle, *Nothing* worked. I was afraid to refuse because of his heart condition—so I gave notice at work, sold our house & all that was in it that the children could not use. Then I went into depression. I was experienced enough to have the sense to go to a *good* psychiatrist who was on our staff. He gave me anti depression pills that were non addictive and we went over all the pitfalls of retirement. Somehow, I made it and we started out. I mention this because as each problem came up, I had thought it out and was able to deal with it. For instance, when husband sits and "makes suggestions" as to how I do things in the trailer, I grin & say "Let's trade places today, you do the

housework and I'll sit in that chair and make suggestions!"
That always makes him laugh—he hates housework.

Now I find I *love* this life. No more taxes and bills and
temperamental doctors and employees. I do what I like when I
want to do it. Now the children scold because we don't write
often enough or call often enough—we are treasured parents &
grandparents. We stop as we travel at each child's place for a
couple of weeks and really get to know our grandchildren.
We always park in a camp as near as possible—and what fun
the grandchildren have as they stay over night with Grandma
& Grandpa! We hear all their problems & joys—they range
from 9 months to 17 years of age. We even take the baby to
give Mom & Dad some rest—but really because *we* enjoy the
baby.

We will go to a retirement camp for a month or so in the
south—then we head for some place less structured in the
wilderness—then back to retirement camps. Campers always
take care of each other so I have no fear for my husband
should he become ill. My neighbors are nearer than my
children ever were. We find we are so *busy* that we relish the
stormy days when we catch up on reading and letter writing
and such.

We have our principal money invested and our monthly
retirement checks are mailed directly to our bank into what
we call our trust account. Our son in law pays all our bills
that come in such as car and trailer licenses, insurance and
because of this we can use our credit cards, which cuts down
the amount of travelers checks & cash that we would have to
carry otherwise. . . . We also maintain another checking
account which we use to pay rent at parks and such places
that will take our personal checks. Each month they (son in
law and daughter) send us a complete financial statement.
They also forward all our mail. What freedom!!

Now we will start wending our way north for the summer.
We have friends and relatives from the tip of Texas way north
into Canada. We are royally welcomed at each stop as we are

completely self sufficient. We have our own beds every night—important for old people.

The energy problem worries us some as we are responsible citizens. We don't feel guilty since we use less gasoline now than we did with two cars going to and from work each day. We move only monthly or every two weeks. We use less electricity than we did in our 8 room house. We consider ourselves energy *savers.* I hope that some seasonal allowance will be made for full time RVers if gas rationing comes. If we should be stranded in the north this fall, it would be disastrous as my husband can not tolerate extreme temperatures—either hot or cold. We have no home to "fly" back to the south. We would be forced to sell our paid for trailer, fly south and buy another at inflated price in the south or west. This strikes me as being very unfair after all our years as tax paying and productive citizens.

I find that my husband who was so dictatorial in his attitude previously, now is my devoted slave. I'm the only one he has to "baby" and he's so concerned that I be happy that my slightest wish is his command. With such treatment, it follows that I will do the same for him. We are happier now than we have ever been. That shows how much *I* know! We don't even have arguments—I simply cannot believe this!

Today he is deep sea fishing which I hate. So while it's fun to be alone, I made a big pot of stew for a change—the home made kind, and will have the fishermen for a surprise dinner tonight when they get back. I decided I had made too much so brought each neighbor next to us, a big bowl for lunch. Now I have two new sets of friends—see how it goes? I had fun too because it's almost impossible to make stew for 2 people unless you want to eat stew for days! Remember storage is a problem in trailers—no big freezers. I do the same when I get a hankering for baked beans—campers share with each other.

We've been stuck in the sand with the tide coming in 40 miles from any road. Who pulled us out?—other campers who had 4 wheel drive. We've lost a wheel on our pickup.

Campers helped us to a small town where the whole town turned out to be sure we had everything we needed. After a fast supper and cocktails served by us, no one would take a penny for their help—and we were all the richer for the experience. We find that America is kind and generous.

Last night a trailer of young people had disco music so loud our trailer rattled and we had to be up at 4:00 A.M. But you know, we rather enjoyed it—it reminded us of when our children were teenagers—and soon we were fast asleep. Children fascinate me—where else can you buy such good conversation for a cookie, a piece of candy or an ice cream cone? It keeps our view point young. There will be time enough for griping some day much later!

I don't know if this has helped you but writing has been fun for me. I'll buy your book if I can find it! Do a good job!!

The Holters are full-timers, the ten percent (approximately one million) of RVers who live year round in some kind of recreation vehicle and have no other home. Mrs. Holter's views on RV life and the health of the elderly are confirmed by a letter I recently received from another RVer, Mrs. Gertrude B. Malkmus, writing from Midway, Georgia. She finds "people who live in RVs to be happier, more optimistic and less grumbly because of poor health than the people who live in conventional homes." Would that more retired people were creative enough to get off their rockers and adopt an active life-style! And would that more Americans, like Mrs. Holter, experienced the country as "kind and generous."

Like the Holters and Ernie Beem, most full-timers are likely to be retired or young. But there are also families living full time on the road. Some years ago an apocryphal story made the rounds about a family in Los Angeles which lived on the freeways in their motor home. They parked in the same spot every night. When they awoke in the morning, the wife drove while the husband showered and dressed on the way to work. Afterwards, she dropped the children off at their schools. During the day she shopped and cleaned and then, in the afternoon, picked the children up at school and her husband at work.

Whatever the truth of this story, Kay Peterson, whose family, kids and all, have been living on the road for years, begins *Home Is Where You Park It* like this: "This book is for anyone who has ever heard the call of the open road. If you dream of the day when you can travel . . . [while] still raising children . . . this book will show you how to make your dreams come true."

Mrs. Peterson relates how "When we were forty-three years old, my husband and I, along with our school-age children, moved into an eight-by-twenty-six foot recreational vehicle and became full-time trailerists. During the next six years we worked in twenty-four different states. Yet we found we were better off financially and happier than we had been at any other period of our lives."

The appeal of Mrs. Peterson's book is obvious. If even couples with growing children can live on the open road, anyone can! The Petersons had owned a trailer, which they used weekends and for an annual, two-week vacation. They liked trailer life so much they began to wonder whether it might be possible to live in one full time. At first, they decided to put it off until their youngest child had graduated from high school, they were further along on home mortgage payments, etc. But soon these seemed like excuses. Grabbing life and running with it they decided: why not now? They sold their house and bought a larger trailer.

Since Joe Peterson is an electrician, his work is influenced by seasonal and market pressures anyway. The largest number of employed, full-time RVers are in the construction trades; they follow job opportunities wherever they are. Mrs. Peterson argues that recessions don't hurt these "boomers" or "tramps" as she calls them, because they can always leave places where opportunities are scarce and move to ones where they are plentiful.

Much of *Home Is Where You Park It* details how the Petersons have gone about solving the challenges of everyday life on the road—from driver license renewals to drug prescriptions to mail.

Sometimes these problems are more complicated than for people who stay in one place. But sometimes, they are *less* complicated or even avoidable. If things get difficult, Mrs. Peterson has a solution: "Your real asset is the wheels under your house. If you encounter regulations you cannot live with, there are other places where officials are more liberal in enforcing laws that were never written for a mobile society." Like the immigrants and pioneers who founded this country, the Petersons believe that if you don't like it where you are, go somewhere else.

The main problem for the Petersons has been school for the children. Their solution has been to move no more than once a semester. Mrs. Peterson doesn't think her children are getting an inferior education by changing schools so often. Quite the contrary, she thinks they are broadened by life on the road and by experiencing different approaches to learning. On their emotional state, she has this to say: "As for that notion about nomadic children being insecure, both Joe and I believe that children do not find security simply because they live in a house that has a solid foundation under it. They find it, rather, in the togetherness of a loving family."

She may have a point. Americans assume that living in one place is good for you, gives you roots. But as John Steinbeck suggests in *Travels with Charlie,* roots is a relatively modern concept in human history. "Perhaps," he writes, "we have overrated roots as a psychic need." The RV industry thinks so. In a recent report they argued that "RVs have probably done more to bring families back together than any other new product." Do any groups have closer family structures than Gypsies or Bedouins? Is it possible that the very permanence and security of a more settled life makes members of families less interdependent, less close?

Kay Peterson also feels that the very transiency of RV campgrounds fosters "old fashioned friendships" between different families. "The trailer park of today," she feels, "is providing the same kind of community life once found in small towns."

Kay Peterson has an interesting theory going: that transiency sometimes *creates* community. She has a bone to pick with books like George W. Pierson's *The Moving American,* Vance Packard's *A Nation of Strangers,* and Robert Weidenbierg's *Corporate Wives— Corporate Tragedies.* These books maintain that mobility and alienation are inextricably linked. Extending their ideas, RVs would be seen as the ultimate in escapism and anti-communitarianism. But the key factor, Peterson feels, is whether one travels by choice or because one has to. "When traveling is *your* idea, it's a lot different than when it's the company's." Also, as she points out, "R.V. families take their homes with them; they are not uprooted. R.V. families live with a built-in assumption that they *will* move and, instead of it being a shock to their systems, they look forward to it." From Peterson's point of view, nomads shouldn't apologize for their life-style; they should tout it.

In their travels, the Petersons have met so many full-timers that they recently organized them into a club called Escapees. It has a newsletter by that name that comes out regularly, and it organizes rallies—called Escapades—year round in different parts of the country. With her club activities, her book, and her regular column in the magazine, *Woodall's Trailer & RV Travel,* Kay Peterson not only lives on the road but has carved a profession for herself out of that life.

Another woman, Janet Dailey, practices her writing craft full time on the road. She writes ten novels a year, mostly enormously popular Harlequin romances. Twenty-four million copies of her books have been sold. Janet and her husband Bill live in a thirty-one-foot Airstream trailer, which has a living room, kitchen, rear bedroom, and bath. They log some thirty thousand miles a year.

Bill Dailey owned a construction business, but his plan was to retire from it by the time he reached forty-five. When he sold the business five years ago, Janet began writing and they hit the road. Bill helps Janet with research, serves as her agent, and is family cook.

Janet sets her alarm for 4:00 A.M. and begins writing immediately in the living room of the trailer. She turns out eleven pages a day—usually by noon. The rest of the day the Daileys can spend as they wish—on the road or visiting the area where they are camping. Usually the Daileys are completely footloose, going wherever whim takes them, but there are a few places in the country they like to visit regularly. Each year they show up at the KOA campground in Rockport, Texas to spend the Christmas holidays with similarly nomadic friends. During a recent visit they explored the Gulf Coast, which became the setting for one of Janet's novels. Janet has yet to write a romantic novel which takes place in an RV campground—though she has thought of it.

A full-time RV life-style seems made to order for some people in the arts. One couple travels about the country doing photographic work. They have a built-in darkroom on their converted bus and, so, are able to deliver finished work in a matter of hours. Another couple, who took early retirement, largely support their motor-home life through crafts—he making jewelry, she weaving—working whenever they choose and setting up their "store" wherever they stop.

Jon Marshall and Sally Squitieri feel that "being on the road is essential to our creativity." Jon is a wildlife artist and carpenter-toymaker, Sally a herbalist and dancer. They call their combined enterprise Gypsy Crafts, and they pursue it in their cedar home which Jon built onto a 1950 Chevrolet flatbed truck. With the aid of a midwife, Jon delivered Sally's baby, Akia, who travels with them—along with two dogs, two cats, and a parrot named Jude—in what Sally calls "Our Noah's Ark on wheels."

Full-timers support themselves in ways other than the construction trades and the arts. Many follow the seasons—buying items wholesale in one area of the country and selling them retail in a part of the country where they are novelties. Flea markets and farmers' markets throughout the country are full of RVers selling everything from pantie hose to antiques. Don Bridges, a native of Maine who was a structural steel worker

Akia helping Jon Marshall and Sally Squitieri build their "Noah's Ark on wheels."

before he got seriously hurt, now supports himself and his wife Jody by selling Mexican wrought-iron objects out of his fifth wheel in Maine in the summer and Maine handicrafts as he passes through Texas on his way to Mexico in the winter.

A number of full-timers find they can make a living as independent sales representatives. One couple in their thirties, originally from San Diego, live in style year round in an expensive Newell motor home, supporting themselves by selling French cookware at the two dozen or so RV rallies they attend each year. With an RV, a salesman doesn't just carry samples of what he sells; he can carry half a truckload of goods (the other half being his home).

David Henry, a traveling representative for Kirsch Company of Sturgis, Michigan, a drapery-equipment manufacturer, travels around his sixty-city territory in the Southeast in a thirty-one-foot motor home towing a small car behind. When he comes to a city, he finds a campsite or pulls into a shopping center parking lot. Then he unhooks his automobile and begins to call on clients. When he first told Kirsch that he would be operating out of a motor home, they were less than enthusiastic. They didn't want "any damn gypsies representing this company." But when Henry was able to show his company that he would save them thousands of dollars in airplane tickets, car rentals, and living expenses, they supported the idea. Now there are hookups for Henry's motor home behind the company warehouse in Atlanta, Georgia.

What Henry particularly likes about RVing about the country "is that I can spend each night in my own bed"—no small feat for a traveling salesman. Also, he doesn't have to worry about finding accommodations, making travel reservations, or having to eat out constantly. Since he's on the road anyway, Henry can choose the best in services along the way—including expert routine mechanical work on his motor home. When he needed a gallbladder operation, he drove to the Duke Medical Center in Durham, North Carolina because of their reputation for medical care. When his hospital roommate began hallucinating, Henry, in order to get some rest, sneaked out of the hospital and spent the night in his familiar motor home bed in the parking lot, returning to his hospital room in the morning.

One of the most difficult things for RVers is making the decision to go full time. They are afraid they cannot survive financially, will be cutting themselves off from loved ones, will encounter dangerous situations on the road, or will find themselves with too much free time on their hands. A letter to *Trailer Life* magazine illustrates the dilemma:

I am under 40 years old and my wife is 35. We have a 13-year old boy living at home. Two years ago we sold all our possessions, except what we could get into our 23-foot travel trailer and spent three months traveling. We loved it and are now interested in exploring seriously the possibility of full time trailering. We would purchase a considerably larger unit than we had before. I have an income but it would not be quite enough for this type of life. Do you know where we could obtain a variety of information on income possibilities as well as on how schooling is handled for children, etc.?

Another letter to the same magazine presents a different range of problems:

Our kids are grown and we are ready and waiting for the day. For many years now we have enjoyed our RV and would dearly love to join the full-timers. Unfortunately, I am 56 years old and Mary is 55. The soonest we could draw any social security would be in five years when Mary reaches 60. Mine would be a year later when I am 62. That seems like such a long time when you are just waiting and champing at the bit. Unlike many people who have worked for a government or company or have a military pension, . . . I will have no pension, per se. All we have is what we will get from social security, some savings, and a very modest amount from investment. We will have to find some way to earn money part time or on the side so we can full-time the rest of the year. Do you have any advice for those in our position?

To answer this kind of letter, *Trailer Life* ran an article called
"How to Start Full Time Trailering 90 Days From Next
Monday." The gist of the article is that virtually anyone can get
into full-time RV life almost immediately with careful planning.
It points out that "the full timer avoids such fixed costs as taxes,
utilities, general upkeep, commuting, house payments and so
on," so that it would be possible for a couple to live on the road
for as little as $100 or even $50 a week.

One difficulty full-timers sometimes run into is antagonism to
their life-style. They are not working (or, at least, not in a
conventional sense), while the people they meet along the way
usually are. While some admire full-timers for their pluck,
others consider them "gypsies," "no account," "poor white
trash," perhaps even dangerous. Subconsciously, some may
associate them with the likes of Perry Smith, one of the
murderers in Truman Capote's *In Cold Blood.* Smith's deprived
background included full-time RVing with his father, a failed
rodeo cowboy, after his mother, an alcoholic, had left them:

> That summer Dad built a primitive sort of trailer, what he
> called a "house car." It had two bunks and a little cooking
> galley. . . . For the next six years we shifted around the
> country. Never stayed nowhere too long. When we stayed
> some place too long, people would begin to look at Dad, act
> like he was a character. . . . So I was glad when we moved
> on.

Some antagonists to RV full-timers regard them as freeloaders.
And a full-timer I met in Florida would, by his own attitudes,
confirm this judgement. "I'll pay my federal taxes because I have
to," he said, "but I'll be damned if I pay any kind of local taxes
or property taxes. I bought this rig to get away from that crap."
Richard G. Rubino, a professor of urban planning at Florida
State University and a part-time camper, thinks there are so
many people living on the road now that their impact on local
governmental services must, at least, be gauged. He warns that in
Sun Belt areas in the winter, local governments may find

themselves overwhelmed by a nomadic population that doesn't pay the taxes that support police, firefighters, the schools, and sanitary services.

Some local constituencies are, nevertheless, as inviting as possible to full-timers, feeling they pay their way through supporting local businesses. "They don't cost us much in the way of services, and they're great for the economy," says Hugh Riley, tax assessor for Cameron County, Texas, a well-frequented wintering area for snowbirds (nomadic Americans who travel about the North in their RVs during the summer and through the South during the winter). "Our doors are open to them."

Our increasingly nomadic population should make things interesting for the Bureau of the Census, which is now endeavoring to count full-time RVers for the first time. The 1980 results may prove startling. Increasing early retirement, the decline of the Protestant work ethic, the influence of the hippie ideal of the 1960s, the growing conviction among some Americans that their country is a rootless one anyway so why not live accordingly, and the increasing sophistication and viability of recreation vehicles have produced a subculture whose numbers, assuming the availability of fuel, are bound to grow.

Chapter IX

Homes on Wheels: The Future

SPEND THE REST OF YOUR LIFE ON WHEELS

An RV Dealer's Sign on State Road 33 in New Jersey

Ah yes, assuming. . . . But that is a mighty big assumption these days, considering the fuel crunches of recent years. In the summer of 1979 gas lines in the Greater New York area extended for blocks, and you could only buy limited quantities every other day. Jimmy Carter delivered a major speech on energy in which he said we were going to squeeze oil out of coal and shale. Maybe so, but it sounded more like blood out of a stone. As this book goes to press, I wonder whether it will eventually be thought of as a description of a vital American subculture or as that subculture's swan song, and whether its appeal will be contemporary or nostalgic ("Yep," says the old man, reading it to his grandchildren, "there really were ve-hickles like that once").

I've been holding back on writing this chapter, not really sure what to say; I have no crystal ball. During the 1979 fuel crisis a network television feature on normally bustling Elkhart asked if it was going to become a ghost town. RV manufacturers around the nation cut back radically on production or temporarily shut down. Campgrounds rented their space by the week or month to RVers staying put for fear of getting stranded on the road. A *New York Times* story headed "Lack of Gas Deprives Campers of Mobility This Summer" described RVers having to mow the grass around their motor homes—a curious greening of America.

If something disagreeable happens once—as when the RV industry was crippled in 1973–1974—it can be dismissed as a fluke. But this time the trouble wasn't the result of a specific oil boycott, and the RV industry has been hurt more than anyone—even more than Detroit. People *need* to drive, but they don't necessarily need an RV. As Chuck Manchester, president of Airstream, once said about the 1973–1974 fuel crisis, "If you can't get gas to go to the grocery store, there isn't much point in buying a trailer." "In our business," John Hanson, president of Winnebago said recently, "the customer has to *know* he can get gas. If not, look out."

The future of the RV industry in America is dependent on one thing: fuel. Without fuel, the industry will die; if there is plenty of fuel, we may all be running around in RVs someday. "This industry was a gold rush in the years before 1973–1974," says Dan Le Hockey, director of the Family Motor Coach Association. "If we could count on fuel, it would be a gold rush again."

Certainly the industry's situation will improve when and if the gas crisis passes. But the long range forecast for RVs will remain cloudy for some time to come.

The Recreation Vehicle Industry Association is trying to keep up enthusiasm for RVs by arguing that fossil fuels are nowhere near being exhausted and that new fuels are on the way. They also are trying to demonstrate that RVs do not use a disproportionate amount of energy. "A lot of people think RVs are firebreathing monsters, but it isn't true," says Bill Garpow, national director for public and legislative affairs of RVIA. "RVs are CVs" (Conservation Vehicles).

Garpow's office distributes a poster headed "Turn Off Your House And Turn On To RVacationing," which claims that an RV consumes as little as twenty percent of the energy consumed by a home and automobile combined. The poster is designed not only to reassure RVers but to disconcert those who, from the comfort of centrally air-conditioned or overheated homes, point to a motor home going by outside and say, "Isn't that obscene?" The fact is, many Americans perceive RVs solely as unnecessary luxury vehicles. It would never occur to them that they might be homes which happen to be on wheels.

An open letter to President Carter from an RVer, which was published in the magazine *Motorhome Life & Camper Coachmen,* presents the other side:

Dear Mr. President:

I'm mad as hell, and I'm not going to take it any more. . . . First, my "gas guzzler," a mini motor home, averages between 9 and 10 miles per gallon. The compact car I bought two years ago, to *save* gas, averages 11 miles per gallon. Is that extra one mpg really "guzzling?"

Next, Mr. President, how about some off-setting credits? When I first heard of your proposal, I decided to keep track of the other energy-using features of my RV. . . . Because our unit's electrical supply is provided by a battery which is charged by the engine, it requires no outside electrical source. During our vacation we used not one kilowatt of electricity.

They tell me you have an engineering background, Mr. President, so I leave the Btu conversion factor to you on the following: during that week, we used 4 gallons of propane for heating and cooking, at a total cost of $2.40. Whatever the Btus, it just figures that when we heat an RV of less than 160 square feet, we require substantially less gas than heating our entire home.

Now, finally, let's compare our actual gasoline usage figures. Had we not taken the vacation, and worked instead, our family's two wage-earners would have driven a total of approximately 400 work-related miles during the week. Even if we both used Detroit's "economy cars," at 11 mpg, we would have purchased 36 gallons of gas.

What I am suggesting, Mr. President, is that the *substantial* resource savings involved in the usage of recreational vehicles merits them applause rather than condemnation.

Resource saving is actually spurring some Americans these days to consider the RV life-style. Mrs. Gertrude Malkmus writes me that "Many retired people are finding that staying in their northern homes is financially impossible now that the price of fuel is so high, and some expect to sell their homes and get a big rig to go south in winter and turn north again for summer."

Whether fuel savers or guzzlers, RVs are a convenient target for American fuel anxieties. Says RVIA's Bill Garpow, "RVs are what Christmas lights were in the winter of 1973–1974." He points to the fact that the Department of Energy excluded RVs from its standby rationing plan—though it later added them after intense lobbying by RVIA.

Trailer Life magazine has had a program underway the past year or so to "prove that RV travel . . . is not unpatriotic." Through its Good Sam Club, *Trailer Life* issues decals to RVers who pledge to conserve energy ten percent by taking fewer trips, going shorter distances, driving at slower speeds, making longer stops, and turning off their gas and electric appliances at home while on the road. The magazine sent a four hundred foot roll of paper to President Carter containing the pledges of thousands of Good Sam members.

These days RV magazines seem to be devoted to only one issue: energy. *Trailer Life* recently ran an article on the energy-conserving RV of the future. This vehicle would be aerodynamically designed, would have a 50–80 MPG orbital engine that would run off virtually any fuel, would have a rooftop wind turbine for electrical production while underway and at windy sites when parked, would have a rooftop solar collector for heating and hot water, and would be totally insulated so as to be cool in summer and warm in winter with minimal energy expenditure.

The industry has already begun to manufacture RVs which use less energy. One motor home is being manufactured with solar panels. Airstream has been making a mini aluminum trailer called Minuet, and there are now tent trailers so light they can be towed by a Volkswagen and still smaller ones that sleep four and can be towed by a motorcycle! Many of the new pickup campers and trailers being manufactured telescope downward while underway to eliminate winddrag. Some micro-mini motor homes get up to 28 MPG. Until recently, the RV industry was challenged to build the largest vehicles that could possibly travel over the American road; now, as the title of a recent RV magazine article puts it, "Small Is In."

In these strivings toward smallness and energy conservation, American RV manufacturers are following in the footsteps of the Europeans, just as Detroit is struggling to catch up to European small car manufacturers. This is ironic because, until recently, America had not only been the center of the RV world; it had virtually *been* the RV world. If Europeans or other foreigners wanted an RV or mobile home, they had to import it from the United States. But just as other typically American products, such as jeans and soft drinks, have been universally adopted by

Europeans, so RVs have made considerable inroads in recent years. Today, there are small RV and mobile home manufacturers in several European countries.

American manufacturers have been attending the few European RV expositions to pick up ideas, and American RV magazines have been inviting European RVers to write for them. Chris Park, an English journalist writing for *Trailer Life* magazine, described America as the "Land of the Giants," explaining that "In the US, monster distances have bred monster vehicles." European RVs, he pointed out, do not have the self-containment of American RVs; they rarely have bathrooms, holding tanks, or much in the way of appliances or sophisticated gadgets. Nor are European campgrounds equipped with hookups for complex RVs. Tony Bradford, editor of Britain's *The Caravan* magazine, tells of traveling about Europe in an American Winnebago and feeling "rising panic . . . in some of the remoter parts . . . where an electric hookup was not available, the battery was fast running down, and the holding tank was fast filling up, with nowhere to empty it other than to back up to the bushes when no one was looking and pull the plug."

While there is an accent on energy conservation and downsizing in American RVs these days, the smallest of American RVs still surpasses European RVs in comfort and flexibility. Also, as if to cover all bets, the American RV industry hasn't given up its love for gadgetry and bigness by a long shot— even with the fuel crisis. Recently, the Dreamer Company began manufacturing what is surely the largest family recreation vehicle in history, the Arctic Sun—a fantastic forty-foot fifth wheel with a unique tow vehicle combining properties of a pickup truck and a motor home. The tow vehicle itself has a mini galley and sleeping facilities so that one can travel self-contained in it even when disengaged from the huge trailer.

But there is something far more extravagant than the Arctic Sun now on the American highway. It's called The Snoozer, and it is a $600,000, sixty-foot, two-story structure consisting of two cars joined by an accordion-like hinge. It is as if someone had fantasied a train off its tracks and onto the highway. Actually, The Snoozer is not a home on wheels; it's a mobile hotel. It rents its eight rooms at $75–$100 a day per person, double occupancy, including breakfast, primarily to golfers and skiers who spend long weekends trying out different courses and slopes without having to worry about accommodations, meals, or driving. Travel between stops takes place at night, while guests sleep. Each room contains two beds, a shower and toilet, a radio, a closed-circuit television, closet, dresser, heating, and air conditioning. There is also a lounge and a bar. Large groups—families, clubs, rock bands—rent Snoozers at $1200 a day.

Another, rather startling, innovation in the RV world is the Coachhouse, a modular home designed to interface with motor homes up to thirty-five feet in length. The idea for such a structure originated with Carl Watts, of Loveland, Ohio, who was concerned about how often his motor home sat outside, unused. In addition to sheltering it, he wished to utilize his motor home's facilities year round—not just when he was on the road. The house is designed so that the motor home can be driven into it, thereby overcoming restrictive parking ordinances. Then the motor home is hooked up and becomes an integral part of everyday living—an extra bedroom, second bath, a spare kitchen, a noisefree lounge area secluded from the rest of the house. Should there be a power failure, the motor home's generator can be used to power the whole house. Coachhouses cost between $20,000 and $30,000 and are being marketed in designed communities—so that RV people will have other RVers as neighbors. While one marvels at how recreation vehicles imitate homes in their design and facilities, here is a home that conforms to the design and facilities of a recreation vehicle. It underscores my earlier statement that "in America there is a less distinct line between what is home and what is motor vehicle than in older, more traditional societies where homes are rooted in the soil."

Recently, *The Futurist* magazine had a cover story called "Recreation Vehicles: A Fantasy" in which it poked fun at recreation vehicles by showing the extremes of which they may be capable. Among the "RVs of the future" it pictured were The Snowmohome, a snowmobile which sleeps four, an amphibious RV in the shape of a duck, and a mountain-climbing RV. Amusing as these "proposals" are, one has only to remember Winnebago's abortive attempts to market a Heli-home to know that they are not so farfetched as to be totally discountable.

But again, it all comes back to fuel. If we don't have sufficient fuel, will there be any recreation vehicle industry at all? If we don't have fuel, will there be a radical restructuring of our society? If we don't have fuel, will there be a transformation of the American character? Without fuel, what is to become of what Vernis Meyer described as "the movingest cusses I ever saw?"

You'll recall Vernis as the fellow I met up in the hills above Steamboat Springs, Colorado. Just before we parted I asked him what he expected to do with his rig when and if the energy situation got real bad. He said he was concerned about it, but not overly. "You can do just about anything to Americans," he said, "but you can't take away their wheels." Dan Le Hockey, director of the Family Motor Coach Association, also said something like that to me: "Americans are a good spirited people. But cut down on their free movement and there may be a revolution."

Sounds ominous. Will Americans, who equate mobility with freedom, become a crazed species as gasoline runs out? Or will they adapt, become less dynamic, more European really, slowly recognizing the finite character of resources as they came to recognize the finite character of their political and military power through the Vietnam experience? Or is this just a dark chapter in the history of American mobility, a lull before the discovery of ample new fuel sources or the appearance of new fuels that will make it possible for Americans to hit the road in RVs whenever they choose into the indefinite future?

The other day I drove past the "SPEND THE REST OF YOUR LIFE ON WHEELS" sign that is the epigraph of this chapter. I got out of the car to look at it, realizing, with a start, that only the sign was there. There were no RVs for sale. The RV dealer had apparently gone out of business or moved. There was just the sign by the edge of the highway, like a lost totem, and, beyond it, weeds slowly covering the asphalt.

As I stood there forlornly, along the highway came a motor home with a Texas license plate, country music coming through the windows. It pulled off next to my car, and out stepped a middle-aged couple dressed in matching cowboy/cowgirl duds. They stood next to me a long time, the three of us just looking up at that sign. It felt like a wreath-laying ceremony.

Then the man brightened, cleared his throat and said, "Well, I *sure* intend to." And the woman said, "*I* sure intend to too." Then she took his arm, and he helped her back up into the motor home. The engine fired, and the country music came back on, something about trucks and mothers and broken hearts. As they pulled out I started to wave—only it came out more like a salute.

Suggested Readings

A complete bibliography of books and articles on RVs and mobile homes would be book length. What follows is a short list of books I found valuable, or enjoyable, or both. Those with extensive bibliographies are noted. I have also provided a list of sources for other information on RVs.

Books

Byam, Wally. *Trailer Travel Here and Abroad.* New York: David McKay, 1960.

> Wally Byam's book offers the most complete discussion available of trailer life and of the Airstream "cult."

Cook, Terry, and Williams, Jim. *Vans and the Truckin' Life.* New York: Harry N. Abrams, 1977.

> A richly illustrated, raunchy advertisement for vanning. Not much on text, but it has a fine bibliography of vanning literature.

Cowgill, Donald Olen. *Mobile Homes: A Study of Trailer Life.* Philadelphia: University of Pennsylvania Press, 1941.

> This early work, originally a Ph.D. dissertation in sociology, emphasizes the social stratification of mobile-home residents. Its bibliography is important for its sources on the early development of the trailer/mobile home in America.

Drury, Margaret J. *Mobile Homes: The Unrecognized Revolution in American Housing.* New York: Praeger, 1972.

> This is probably the most authoritative one-volume discussion of mobile homes as housing to date. It has a fine bibliography.

Edwards, Carlton M. *Homes for Travel and Living: The History and Development of the Recreational Vehicle and Mobile Home Industries.* East Lansing: Carl Edwards, 1977.

> This is the only omnibus work on the RV and mobile home industries. It is a compendium of facts and charts and bibliography— really a reference work rather than a book to be read cover to cover. Edwards was at one time a professor of mobile-home-industry education at Michigan State University, and he has served as historian of the Recreation Vehicle/Mobile Home Hall of Fame.

Edwards' book is published privately and is available from him at 2672 Greencliff Dr., East Lansing, Michigan 48823.

Gartner, John. *All about Pickup Campers, Van Conversions and Motor Homes.* Beverly Hills: Trail-R-Club of America, 1969.

This book deals enthusiastically with the three types of RVs mentioned in the title. It has a wealth of photographs of early RVs.

Johnson, Sheila K. *Idle Haven.* Berkeley: University of California Press, 1971.

The most interesting reading of the books available on mobile home life. Johnson concentrates on life in a particular mobile home park near San Francisco.

Lidz, Jane. *Rolling Homes: Handmade Houses on Wheels.* New York: A & W Publishers, 1979.

A gorgeous book of color photographs of do-it-yourself homes on wheels—most of them made from trucks and buses. Basically a coffee table book, *Rolling Homes* has almost no text, but it makes up for it with the richness of the architectural detail in its photographs.

Meloan, Taylor W. *Mobile Homes: The Growth and Business Practices of the Industry.* Homewood, Ill.: Richard D. Irwin Publishers, 1954.

This book is particularly strong on the early history of the trailer/mobile home. It has a pretty fair bibliography also.

Pallidini, Jodi, and Dubin, Beverly. *Roll Your Own: The Complete Guide to Living in a Truck, Bus, Van or Camper.* New York: Macmillan, Collier Books, 1974.

A *Whole Earth Catalog* approach to RV life. Basically, it tells how to build, maintain, and live in a homebuilt hippie truck or bus.

Peterson, Kay. *Home Is Where You Park It.* Chicago: Follett, 1977.

Home Is Where You Park It is the best book available on the joys and problems of full-time RV living on the road.

Steinbeck, John. *Travels with Charlie.* New York: Viking, 1962.

This is Steinbeck's nonfiction treatment of his travels around the United States in a pickup camper with his dog Charlie. A charming book that evokes the poetic side of life on the road in an RV.

Stephen [Stephen Gaskin]. *The Caravan.* New York: Random House, 1972.

The Caravan is a series of interviews offered, and religious services conducted, by Stephen during several months in late 1970 and early 1971 when he traveled through America with a caravan of some fifty bus-homes of young people. The caravan became the nucleus of The

Farm commune in Summertown, Tennessee, which Stephen serves as spiritual leader.

Wolman, Baron. *Vans: A Book of Rolling Rooms.* Garden City, N.J.: Doubleday, 1976.

A coffee table book of color photos of van exteriors and interiors.

Other Materials

The largest publisher of RV and mobile-home books in the world is the Trail-R-Club of America, Box 1376, Beverly Hills, California 90213. These are mainly how-to books (e.g., *How to Buy Recreational Vehicles; This Wonderful World of Mobile Home Living*), but Trail-R also publishes histories of the industry, cartoon books on RV life, and many novelty items. Trail-R will send a free catalog on request.

For current information on the RV industry and RV life the best sources are the myriad magazines that are published regularly and have wide circulations. I list below some of the most popular ones.

Custom Vans, published monthly by Twentieth Century Publications, P.O. Box 547, Chatsworth, California 91311.

During the seventies, dozens of van magazines appeared. *Custom Vans* has the widest circulation and the most attractive presentation.

Family Motor Coaching, published monthly by the Family Motor Coach Association, P.O. Box 44144, Cincinnati, Ohio 45244.

As discussed earlier, the FMCA is composed exclusively of owners of bus conversions and large motor homes. Articles in the magazine concentrate on these vehicles.

Motorhome Life, published monthly by Trailer Life Publishing Company, 23945 Craftsman Rd., Calabasas, California 91302.

This is the only RV magazine dealing exclusively with all kinds and sizes of motor homes. The Trailer Life Publishing Company is the largest publisher of RV periodical literature, with six magazines coming out regularly.

Trailer Life, published monthly by Trailer Life Publishing Company, 23945 Craftsman Rd., Calabasas, California 91302.

Trailer Life is the oldest continuously published RV magazine and has the largest circulation. It is a general magazine dealing not just with trailers but with every type of RV. The Trailer Life Company sponsors the Good Sam Club, the largest club of RV owners unassociated with a particular brand or type of RV.

Woodall's Trailer & RV Travel, published monthly by Woodall
Publishing Company, 500 Hyacinth Place, Highland Park, Illinois
60035.

Woodall's is another general RV magazine with wide circulation, and
it is produced by the other major publisher of the RV industry. In
addition to this magazine, the Woodall Company publishes
campground directories and annual catalogs keyed to RV life.

For a wealth of RV brochures on every conceivable subject, write to
the Recreation Vehicle Industry Association, 14650 Lee Rd., Chantilly,
Virginia 22021. For similar materials on mobile homes, write to the
Manufactured Housing Institute, 1745 Jefferson Davis Highway,
Arlington, Virginia 22022. Finally, all RV and mobile-home
manufacturers provide brochures about their products, and some of the
larger ones publish materials which go beyond the strictly commercial
(e.g., *Motor Home Buyer's Guide,* by Ginny Ade, published by and
available from Winnebago Industries, Forrest City, Iowa 50436).

Index